THE
MOTORCYCLIST'S
GUIDE TO
SCOTLAND

Published by
Tarmap Press
Bridgend
Wamphray
Moffat
DG10 9NA
www.tarmap.co.uk
ISBN: 978-1-9996357-0-1
A catalogue record for this book is available from the British Library

Designed and typeset by www.revocreative.co.uk
Printed and bound by Pozkal.

THE MOTORCYCLIST'S GUIDE TO SCOTLAND

THE MOTORCYCLIST'S GUIDE

ACKNOWLEDGEMENTS

It's easy to get into debt on a project like this and I managed it very quickly. I owe a great debt to Joe Philipsz at Rentamotorcycle.co.uk, part of Motorrad Central Scotland, the BMW motorcycle dealership in Edinburgh. With my own bike unsuitable, I needed some wheels for a research trip. Joe's enthusiasm was immediate, his support was generous and the R 1200 RS he provided was ideal!

A belated thank you to Alistair Martin who spotted me sobbing at the roadside after I lost the fob for the 'keyless ride' BMW. He was too polite to say so, but I'm sure he would have enjoyed the run through Glenshee much more without me riding pillion, leaning out to search the verges. Thanks are due to my sister, Henny – always ready to help in a crisis – who raced up from Killiecrankie to join me for a fob hunt in vain and a lunch in Braemar. I am grateful to Motorrad Central Scotland's Martin Williamson for giving up a day off to carry a replacement fob up the A93 to get me back on the road that same afternoon. Martin, an experienced motorcycle tour leader, also cast his eye over parts of this book during the production process, offering invaluable advice and generously sharing his knowledge.

I'm grateful to those fellow bikers who allowed me to use their photographs on routes where mine were either inadequate or absent. Particularly John Herbin – a.k.a. Kamchat – who was killed in a road accident in Argyll in April 2018. He died doing what he loved but is greatly missed by his family, friends and many followers on the Adventure Riders forum. Several former colleagues in BBC Scotland kept me right on the pronunciation of place names, and many friends and biking acquaintances shared their recommendations for routes, cafés and accommodation.

I am indebted to cartographer Helen Stirling, who created the maps to illustrate the routes. If you need the services of a map-maker, Helen is a joy to work with. If this book is readable, it is due in no small part to Phil Hunt of Textbookfinish for his sterling work as copy-editor and proofreader. And if it is easy on the eye, it is entirely due to my friend and collaborator David McNeill of Revocreative who is responsible for the layout and design. Finally, I am indebted to my long-suffering family, particularly my wife Annie. Although no fan of motorbikes, she doesn't begrudge me bike-time and, so far at least, she has always been here when I get back!

Thank you all.

HONOURABLE MENTIONS
(AND BACK-SCRATCHING OBLIGATIONS)

The production of this book would have been a more difficult process without the involvement of the following:

Motorrad Central Scotland, Edinburgh's BMW dealership, were the first people I approached when embarking on this venture and their enthusiasm and support encouraged me to go ahead with it. I was grateful for the use of a bike from their hire fleet but their belief in the project itself was just as important. If you're planning to hire a motorbike in Scotland, I wholeheartedly recommend them. They have a wide range of latest-plate BMWs for hire, and a refreshing attitude to customers and customer service. The bill for a lost key fob and some slight pannier damage was eye-wateringly small; the policy for all hire-bike repairs is parts at cost and no labour charges! They hire (and sell) motorcycles and arrange tours. It's a cliché but their work really does seem to be their hobby. In the spirit of full disclosure, they gave me the use of a bike for three weeks in return for "a mention" in the book. www.rentamotorcycle.co.uk

Motorcycle Diaries, inspired by – but not to be confused with – the Che Guevara book, is an on-line database of great roads to ride. Originally set up by people involved in researching locations for car and motorbike commercials, the itinerary app is a growing, global library of wonderful roads, simply explained and illustrated. Peer-to-peer road sharing, inspiring epic road trips and encouraging us all to get out there and explore – just as Che did in the 1950s. In return for the use of some images, they asked us to point people towards their website. www.motorcycle-diaries.com

Erik Peters is a journalist and motorcycle traveller based in Cologne. His video *Highlands & Islands; Where Scotland's Heart Beats Loudest* documents a solo trip to Scotland he made in 2015. Originally made for the German market, the American voice-over misses the target with some pronunciations and his diet is a little suspect but the video serves as a fine introduction for those yet to visit Scotland. Erik allowed me to use his pictures in return for a plug for the video. Available from Amazon as a DVD or download.

ROUTE FINDER

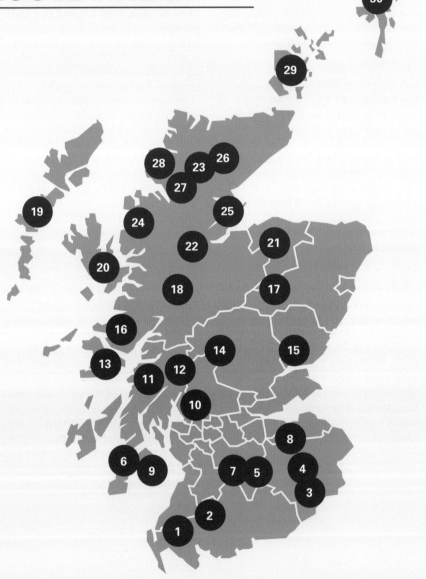

CONTENTS

THE MOTORCYCLIST'S GUIDE TO SCOTLAND

There's nothing quite like riding a motorcycle. Whether it's a short run after work, a day's outing with friends or a long-distance tour, there's something about riding a motorbike that makes us feel more alive.

And when you can do it in Scotland – with empty roads, glorious scenery and hospitable locals – well, it's hard to think of a better place to be than on a motorbike in the Scottish countryside. This book aims to help you experience the joys of motorcycling while exploring the wonders of Scotland.

Many visitors think Scotland begins in Edinburgh and ends in Inverness.

Remarkably few head to the south of Scotland, where some of the country's best biking roads can be found. Only the more enterprising take a ferry to explore the islands to the west or north. Even those who travel to the Highlands tend to squeeze themselves onto the busy highways, like the A9 – a lovely road ruined by traffic. Thank goodness they don't know any better! It leaves treasures like the old A93 from Perth to Braemar free for the rest of us. Irish ferry traffic thunders along the A75

through Galloway, leaving the network of glorious byways and country lanes for those of us for whom the journey is as important as the destination.

Scotland might be a small country but it's a big place. It attracts millions of visitors each year, but it's still relatively easy to find peace and isolation. Conversely, it's not hard to find good company if that's what you want, in pubs, campsites, street corners, in fact anywhere you choose to stop and strike up a conversation. There are budget hostels and budget-busting hotels, roadside cafés and gourmet restaurants just around the corner. History, scenery,

hospitality, music, wildlife, food, festivals… Scotland is a country full of colour, culture and tradition. It's waiting to be explored and there's no better way to explore it than on a motorbike.

The suggestions in these pages will help you get the most out of the roads, whether it's a classic route in the West Highlands or a little-known country lane in the Borders. The major cities – Glasgow, Edinburgh, Dundee and Aberdeen – don't get much of a mention; we're concentrating on smaller communities and open roads. If you detect a bias towards the west of Scotland, that's because it has more of the best roads! You won't always be alone; some routes can be busy, but they are still worth the effort. The routes in this book range from under 90 miles to over 500, which equates to a couple of hours to a couple of days in the saddle, with the tour lasting several days. Along the way, we've recommended things to see and places to stop. We hope the ideas and suggestions in these pages will serve not just as a guide, but as an incentive for those who want to fire up their motorbikes and hit the road.

TOURING IN SCOTLAND

WHAT TO BRING ALONG FOR THE JOURNEY

Like a good Boy Scout, motorcyclists in Scotland should 'Be Prepared' – be prepared for poor weather, bad luck and midges. Scottish weather is certainly changeable and a sunny day can turn wet very quickly. Most local bikers won't cross town without waterproof clothing, let alone cross the country. Make sure you pack a decent set of waterproofs and several layers of warm, base layer clothing. You'll be riding in remote parts of the country so carry a tool kit for minor breakdowns, some cable ties and electrical tape. If you are riding an older machine, consider packing a set of replacement cables and bulbs. A spare key is not a bad idea either, just in case!

It is always advisable to have a puncture repair kit and to know how to use it – you don't want to be working it out in fading light, surrounded by midges in some remote glen, with no phone signal! Take your mobile phone, of course, but don't rely on getting a connection. Signal reception is very patchy in remote areas.

Take this guide with you. The road maps will give you the freedom to investigate alternative routes – if another road looks interesting, ride that one instead. Scotland is a secure and friendly country, with minimal risk to your safety if you get lost. Besides, there is usually a helpful local who can get you back on the right track.

Although we list refuelling stops in the route directions, if you ride a motorcycle with a range of only 100 miles or so on a tank – and especially if you are heading to the northwest of Scotland – it's worth carrying a couple of extra litres in a fuel bottle if you have room. Bring a snack and something to drink. Carry some cash because not everywhere accepts cards. If you are touring, travel as light as you can. Unless you're on a big continent-crosser with cavernous panniers and topbox, you will have to be selective. You'll probably want a phone, charger, map, torch, tools, a first-aid kit, then a fleece, underwear, socks, a change of clothing and your waterproofs. That's probably enough. (As any know-all will tell you, the bike may not carry everything you want, but it'll carry everything you need.) After packing the essentials, be ruthless when it comes to the other stuff. Stow your heaviest items as low on the bike as possible, while keeping the weight evenly distributed on either side. Finally, be methodical. It's a lot easier to find something when you know that you put clothes and toiletries in the left pannier, tool kit, parts and first-aid kit in the right pannier, and your phone, camera and chewing tobacco in the tank bag.

Inspect your motorcycle frequently. Check it in the morning before you start, then again when you stop for coffee, when you fill the tank and before you lay it up for the night. You can't check it too often. Look out for oil or coolant leaks, a loose chain, sprocket damage, worn cables, loose fixtures or luggage and anything that looks out of place. Check tyre pressures and fluid levels regularly. It's corny but true: if you look after your motorcycle, it will look after you.

ACCOMMODATION

Finding somewhere good to stay in Scotland used to be a bit of a lottery unless you had deep pockets. Things have changed in recent years and Scotland now has plenty of great accommodation across the price range, from budget hostels right up to exclusive hotels. There are still some horror stories, but these are fewer nowadays and it is easier to check places online before booking. The options in remoter corners are reduced over the winter when many establishments close down. A hotel will usually offer breakfasts, lunch and dinner and have a licenced bar. Although you can generally expect a hearty breakfast when staying in a guesthouse or B&B, you will probably have to eat elsewhere in the evening, although some provide evening meals by prior arrangement. For hotels, guesthouses and even B&Bs, it's worth checking that the price quoted includes breakfast. When booking any of them, check whether the tariff is for the room or per person. The number of hostels and bunkhouses in Scotland seems to be growing and these days you won't have to go too far off your route to find a hostel offering budget accommodation

and often convivial company. You probably won't get breakfast, but they usually provide somewhere where you can make your own (if you supply the food). In certain parts of the country such as Skye and along the NC500, it is essential to book your accommodation in advance. The further ahead you book, the easier it gets to find a bed.

CAMPING

If you want the convenience of showers and toilets, there is likely to be a good campsite close to your route, though again it's worth pre-booking during the height of the season. On the other hand, if you want to find your own spot to pitch a tent, you're perfectly free to do so. Wild camping – that is camping in the countryside at large – is legal under the Scottish Land Reform Act of 2003. Just as people enjoy the 'right to roam' in Scotland, so campers are free to spend the night under canvas on most unenclosed land. The rules are pretty straightforward:

- Don't camp in fields, near houses, farms or historic structures.
- Don't stay in one spot for long – three nights at the most.
- Don't camp in large groups or over-crowd a location.
- Use a stove rather than light a camp fire and remove all trace of the fire if you do light one.
- Don't cut down or damage trees in your search for fuel.
- Take a trowel so you can bury your 'deposits'.
- Leave no trace that you were there – take your litter to a bin (and it's good to pick up litter left by others if you can).

Wild camping is not allowed in the Loch Lomond and Trossachs National Park, where special rules about camping were introduced in 2017. Between March and September, Camping Management Zones come into force to protect the busiest areas. Campers must use an official campsite or buy a permit to camp in the wild. You can find out which areas are restricted and buy permits from the park authorities (www.lochlomond-trossachs.org).

Wherever you camp, make sure you have a tent that can withstand the Scottish winds; a pop-up festival tent probably won't last long in the Highlands! And take a side stand plate (or a paint tin lid) to put under your side stand on soft ground. If you tie a bit of string to it – long enough to reach from the ground to your handlebars – you can drop the plate when you arrive, loop the loose end round the bars and recover it easily when you leave.

MIDGES, TICKS AND CLEGGS

No one visits Scotland without dire warnings about the perils of the midge ringing in their ears. In the words of the song: "Wi' teeth like piranhas, they drive you bananas." The warnings should not put you off, but nor should they be ignored. Midges certainly thrive in Scotland's humid and temperate climate, but no midge can keep up with a motorbike. It's only when you stop that the problems begin. Whether it is erecting a tent, tightening a chain or taking a leak, anything that happens outdoors can become a midge-induced nightmare.

Practise 'safe sightseeing' by wearing protection. Apparently the Royal Marines (among others) use Avon 'Skin So Soft' to keep the midges at bay. Many people find Jungle Formula or Smidge effective. Whatever your choice, don't set foot in the Highlands without a plentiful supply of some kind of midge repellent. And head to a fishing tackle shop, or search online, to buy an anti-midge head net, or better still a complete bodysuit. Your companions might laugh when you put it on, but pretty soon they'd probably trade their motorbike for it.

While midges are simply annoying, ticks can have more serious consequences. These tiny, spidery beasties lurk in long grass, bracken and heather waiting to attach themselves to something living so they can drink its blood. Some – not all – are infected by Lyme disease, which can cause significant problems in humans. Why are we telling you this? Well, if you're camping, picnicking or answering a call of nature then you are a target. If you need to go into the bracken for privacy (armed with a trowel and a toilet roll), be careful. Don't let the ticks put you off camping, but be aware of them and take precautions. There is plenty of advice online about prevention and treatment (see page 202).

Cleggs are the bull terrier of the fly world. Gadflies, horse-flies, elephant-flies… call them what you will, these flying bastards have a bite like the kick of a mule but (usually) cause no lasting effects. With cleggs and midges, it's only the female that bites. Make of that what you will.

REFUELLING

Not surprisingly, petrol pumps are thin on the ground in Scotland's remote and rural areas and you should plan accordingly. An increasing number of petrol stations have a 24-hour facility, but don't rely on being able to fill up out of hours in rural areas. In the far northwest and in the Hebrides, you might find the pumps closed on Sundays. Expect to pay more for fuel as you travel further from the centres of population.

THE SINGLE TRACK ROAD

At some point you will find yourself on a single track road, with passing places. Most drivers on single track roads show consideration to motorcyclists by pulling over to let them past, so it is good to show similar consideration to other road users. Here are the conventions.

* If you spot something coming in the opposite direction, adjust your speed to arrive at the nearest passing place at the same time.
* Stop if you arrive at a passing place first.
* Always pull into a passing place on your left. If the passing place is on your right, wait opposite it until the other vehicle goes past.
* Give way to vehicles coming uphill if you can, especially trucks and tractors that take a lot of effort to stop and start.
* Don't travel in a convoy – there may not be enough room in the nearest parking place for you all.
* Never park in a passing place.
* Always acknowledge another's courtesy with a friendly wave.

When you come to a stop on a narrow road, be wary of where you place your foot. The verges are often eroded, and the surface may be far from solid. It's easy to topple!

ROAD HAZARDS

Surface dressing – hot tar sprayed onto the road then sprinkled with chippings – is the scourge of the motorcyclist. Look out for temporary signs warning of surfacing dressing or loose chippings and ride accordingly. Lookout for any build up of gravel in the middle of roads where it's thrown by vehicles' wheels. Cattle grids – especially when wet – should be crossed straight on, and upright!

Be wary of tractors or farm bikes emerging from fields at inopportune moments or parked round a blind corner, or leaving mud on the road near field entrances. It can happen anywhere, but when the roads are remote and little used, farmers tend to let their guard down.

Many roads in rural Scotland are unfenced, and fences are often in a poor condition, so always go into a corner aware that a sheep (or perhaps a Heilan' coo!) may be blocking the road ahead. And watch out for sheep beside the road – they'll decide to cross just when you've passed the braking point. Lambs are particularly skittish! Be careful of puddles which may be hiding interesting potholes. Oh, and never follow a livestock trailer too closely – you never know what might squirt out as you prepare to overtake.

FERRIES

Ferry journeys are almost as much fun as riding a motorbike. They take you to exciting places and the land looks different when viewed from the sea. Sometimes they provide a convenient shortcut, but often they are the only way to visit fascinating places like Mull, Harris or Orkney. On longer routes, you may be required to tie your motorcycle down to the deck. If so, always put your bike on its side-stand rather than the centre stand – three points of contact with the ground are much better than two – and leave the bike in first gear. Don't be tempted to lift your side-stand until the ferry is docked – the shudder when the ferry comes alongside can easily topple a bike. In fact, it is most stable if you stand astride your bike with your foot on

your side-stand, while keeping the bike in gear. Book ahead if you can, especially in peak season, although ferry crews are usually pretty obliging and motorbikes can often be squeezed on even when cars are being turned away. Investigate CalMac's 'Island Hopper' tickets, which can be used on the west coast and Western Isles. They allow you to link several crossings for a lower cost than buying the tickets separately. If you're travelling on the Western Ferries service between Gourock and Dunoon it's much cheaper to buy your tickets before you board the ferry.

MOTORCYCLING IN SCOTLAND

DRINK-DRIVING LAWS

These are stricter north of the border than in other parts of the United Kingdom and driving while under the influence of alcohol (or drugs) is taken very seriously. The legal limit is just 50mg of alcohol in 100ml of blood. There is no safe way to gauge how much you can drink before being over the limit, so the best advice is don't touch the stuff until you have put the bike to bed for the night. And be aware that you could still be over the limit in the morning if you had a heavy night!

SPEED LIMITS

Generally speaking, speed limits are set at 70mph (112kph) on motorways and dual carriageways, 60mph (96kph) on roads outside built-up areas and 30mph (48kph) in towns and villages. If there are street lamps, assume it's a 30mph if you don't see signs to the contrary. Around schools it is common to have a 20mph (32kph) limit indicated by flashing lights on a speed limit sign. Look out for signs indicating the limit for that section of road. If there are no signs, then the national speed limit applies.

FLASHING

Drivers in the UK often use their headlights to communicate with other road users. The Highway Code, the rule book for UK drivers, states that flashed lights should only be used to signal your presence on the road. But drivers have got into the habit of flashing their lights for many reasons: to say 'hello', 'thank you', 'keep out of this gap' or 'come into this gap'. Flashed headlights can be a greeting, a warning, an invitation, a rebuke, an expression of gratitude or an expression of anger. That's why the Highway Code urges us "never to assume (the flashing of lights) is a signal to go. Use your judgment and proceed carefully." Don't trust a flasher!

ACCIDENTS

If you are involved in a road accident that results in injury to a person or animal, or in damage to another vehicle or property, you must stop and remain at the scene for 'a reasonable period of time'. You are obliged to give your details (name & address, ownership details and registration number of your motorcycle, etc) to anyone who has reasonable grounds to ask for them. If you cannot report an accident at the time, you must tell the police about it within 24 hours. If required to do so, be prepared to produce your insurance certificate at the scene or to produce it at a named police station within seven days. You should also report any accident to your insurance company (or rental company) as soon as you can. If you are involved in an accident that wasn't your fault, make sure that you get the names and addresses of witnesses, details of vehicles and people involved, and report the incident to the police.

THE POLICE

Generally, the police in Scotland are not a bad lot. Greet them with a smile, treat them with courtesy and, like most of us, they will respond accordingly. They tend to react less well to abuse and hostility. All road users are obliged to stop if requested to do so by a police officer. Make sure you pull over in a safe place, then wait by your motorcycle and let the officer approach you. If you've committed an offence, the officer should give details of the offence and the action being taken against you. This could range from a gentle warning, to a fixed penalty or even the confiscation of your motorbike. You might be required to produce your documents, or take them to a named police station within seven days. It is an offence to refuse to take a breathalyser test if the police ask you to. It is prudent to make a note of the officer's badge number and ask where they are based.

SECURITY

Scotland is a safe country to visit, and the Scots are a warm-hearted and honest people. But wherever you travel, it is sensible to take reasonable precautions when leaving your motorbike and luggage unattended. In Scotland, when parking overnight in towns, or by main roads, enable any alarms and security devices. This is particularly important in Edinburgh, where instances of motorcycle theft are alarmingly common – be very careful where you leave your bike overnight in Scotland's capital. Choose your accommodation according to the security of the parking arrangements. If you ride an older machine without alarms, and are visiting Edinburgh, only stay where the car park is out of sight of the street and, preferably, locked at night. It is worth paying extra for somewhere with secure parking. In remoter areas, the chances of anyone interfering with your bike are negligible, but it is still advisable to remove keys and ensure valuables are locked away.

EMERGENCY CONTACTS

Carry a note of the telephone number and address of your motorcycle's Scottish dealers. If you have signed up to any breakdown service, or have hired your wheels, keep a note of the relevant numbers to contact in case of emergency. It's unlikely you'll come seriously unstuck on your trip but you should prepare in case you do. Make sure your emergency information and medical conditions are visible in case of an accident. If you need help but are, for some reason, unable to communicate, it's important that people know who to call and what your particular medical requirements might be. Wear a medical bracelet if you have one, or stick an 'emergency data carrier' on your helmet.

HOW SCOTLAND INVENTED MOTORCYCLING (SORT OF)

The British School of Motoring used to have a logo that depicted Great Britain as a car driver: Cornwall had its foot on the pedals; Wales held the wheel; England formed the torso (best not mention Kent); and Scotland was the head, where the brains are kept.

Surprisingly, for a nation with a proud record in engineering and invention, Scotland cannot claim to have invented the motorcycle per se. On the other hand, it did give the world the machine that preceded it – the bicycle. Credit for the first pedal bike goes to Kirkpatrick Macmillan, a young blacksmith from Kier in Dumfriesshire.

In 1839, he made a wooden 'hobby-horse' frame with front-wheel steering and pedals connected by rods to cranks at the rear. It was basic but effective, and he was soon riding the 14 miles from Thornhill to Dumfries in under an hour. Macmillan never tried to patent his invention and copies were soon being sold all over the country.

MACMILLAN'S BICYCLE

Not soon enough, however, for the Scot who invented the inflatable tyre. It wasn't – as most people think – John Boyd Dunlop, but Robert William Thomson from Stonehaven. When he patented his 'aerial wheel' in 1845, he was ahead of his time – by roughly 40 years. Bicycles had only just been invented, so nobody knew they needed tyres!

In 1887, Ayrshire vet John Boyd Dunlop (working in Belfast) made it happen. Within a year of trying his prototype 'pneumatic' tyres on his son's tricycle, 'Dunlops' were winning races and selling like hot cakes.

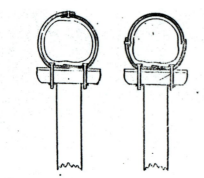

THOMSON'S ÆRIAL WHEEL
[The earliest patented pneumatic tire.]

Thomson sued and lost, so it's Dunlop's name which is synonymous with one of the most famous motoring brands in history. To be fair, Dunlop later acknowledged that he'd actually 're-invented' the tyre but said he'd been unaware of Thomson's device; not unreasonable as he'd only been five years old at the time. Thomson didn't do too badly though; he was a serial inventor with an admirable range that included the first mechanical road haulage vehicle and the fountain pen.

THE DUNLOP BRIDGE AT LE MANS

We should all raise a cheer for John Loudon McAdam, the 19th century engineer who realised that good roads need a proper structure, with a mix of stone sizes and a camber to get rid of surface water.

But 'tarmac' – when tar was poured onto a 'macadamised' road – didn't happen until the early 20th century. County Surveyor (and token Englishman in this chapter) Edgar Hooley came across a stretch of road outside an ironworks in Nottingham where a barrel of tar had fallen off a cart and broken open. Someone had covered the mess with waste slag from the works and, in doing so, had inadvertently invented modern roads. Hooley registered the name Tarmac in 1902 and started the company of the same name. McAdam had been dead for 60 years, but people still think he invented the stuff.

FIRST AMERICAN MACADAM ROAD

There are other Scots who have contributed – directly or indirectly – to our ability to enjoy motorcycling. There's Thomas Telford, the peerless engineer responsible for building countless roads and bridges in the 18th and 19th centuries, almost all of which are still in use today. He is name-checked regularly throughout this book. Glasgow's James Watt invigorated the industrial revolution with his condensing steam engine. David Dunbar Buick – of car company

depressing year for Scotland, but James Goodfellow cheered us all up by inventing the ATM and the PIN number. Where would we be without them?

fame – from Arbroath developed the overhead valve engine from which almost all modern engines are derived. There's Glasgow chemist Charles Macintosh, who sandwiched a layer of rubber between cloth and invented waterproof clothing (or at least the first that didn't smell of wax or wet animal). Alexander Graham Bell came up with the first telephone allowing us to ring to say we'll be late home. James Chalmers from Dundee invented the adhesive stamp allowing us to write to say we're not coming home. James Clerk-Maxwell took the first colour photograph in 1861, while James Dewar patented the first vacuum flask in 1892 to keep our coffee warm. And what ride-out doesn't begin with a hearty breakfast? Give thanks for Edinburgh scientist Alan MacMasters who invented the electric toaster in 1893, and of course, Janet Keiller from Dundee who produced the world's first shredded-peel marmalade to spread on the toast. Finally, 1966 was a thoroughly

Queuing outside the bank, probably. So to conclude, Scots didn't invent the motorbike, but there's an argument to say that they invented practically everything else.

1922 BEARDMORE PRECISION

MOTORCYCLES THAT WERE MADE IN SCOTLAND

Although there have been over a thousand known motorcycle manufacturers in the UK since 1880, very few have been based north of the border. Of those, just one, The Victoria Motor & Cycle Company of Dennistoun (1902–1926), produced bikes in any great number – at its peak it had a range of nine different models, although only a handful of machines are known to have survived. At the other end of the scale were the Dundee-based Christie brothers, who produced just a single motorbike.

In the early days, it was possible to build kits by buying a frame and forks, adding the engine of your choice, wheels and a seat before painting your name on the tank. Does that qualify as a manufacturer? If so, then G.A.C.S. (Glasgow Auto Cycle Services) is another Scottish manufacturer. A surviving example can be found in the Myreton Motor Museum in East Lothian. Also small-scale and short-lived, the Templeton Brothers built Tee Bee motorcycles in Glasgow's Sauchiehall Street in 1910. George Rutherford produced Dunedins in Edinburgh between 1902 and 1910 with a fine example in the collection of the National Museum of Scotland. Clydeside's vast engineering conglomorate William Beardmore and Co. Ltd employed 40,000 people, building everything from cars to ships and aircraft to pre-fab houses. The company dabbled in motorbikes for a few years in the 1920s, building the Beardmore Precision.

The Royal Scot can claim to be entirely Scottish, from the name to the frame. Built in Anniesland in the 1920s, Royal Scots used frames from the Victoria Company with sleeve-valve engines made, just along the road, by Barr & Stroud.

AJR CIGARETTE CARD

Douglas

MOTOR CYCLES
1930.

JOCK PORTER AND HIS NEW GERRARD

successful. He designed, built, raced and won the TT on his 'New Gerrard' machines, with production lasting from 1922 until 1940. One of his motorcycles is in the collection at Glasgow's Riverside Museum, along with examples of the Victoria and Beardmore.

The best-known marque with which Scotland is associated is the Douglas (1907–1956). The company was founded by Scottish brothers William and Edwin Douglas, who moved to Bristol to start a blacksmith and engineering company. By the end of the First World War, the company owned the biggest motorcycle factory in the world, and had supplied 70,000 machines to the War Office. Although all production took place in England, the company remained proud of its Scottish roots. Even today, the logo of the Douglas Motorcycles forum features a cheery chappie in a tartan 'bunnet'.

Most people with an interest in classic bikes know of the AJS, but fewer are aware of the AJR, built in Edinburgh by A.J. Robertson. He launched his range of bikes by riding them, aged 19, in the 1925 TT, but failed to finish in any of the three classes. He completed the circuit in 1926, but was too slow to be of interest, and AJR's short history ended the same year. Jock Porter, also based in the capital, was altogether more

JIMMY GUTHRIE

BRAVEHEARTS IN LEATHERS

The first Scotsman to win at the Isle of
Man was the bike-builder mentioned
above, Jock Porter. He won the
250cc TT in 1923 and the first Ultra-
Lightweight 175cc class in 1924,
leading to international success that
included three Belgian GP victories
and twice becoming European 250cc
champion (at a time when the European
title was effectively the world title).
Arguably the greatest of Scotland's
champions was Jimmy Guthrie, one
of Hawick's favourite sons. His funeral
procession through the town in 1937
is said to have been three miles long.
In the 1930s he was one of the most
successful and popular racers in
Europe. He won the Junior and Senior
double at the 1934 TT, a year later
winning the European Championship
and riding round the concrete bowl at
Monterey on a Norton 500 averaging
114.09 mph. It was so fast he broke
the world 50-km, 50-mile, 100-km and
100-mile records, not only for the 500c
class but in the larger 750cc and
1,000cc classes as well. He

died at the German GP in 1937 aged 40;
leading by two minutes and odds-on to
win his third European Championship,
he crashed on the final lap and was
thrown into trees. Norton blamed the
bike, but another competitor (Stanley
Woods, no less) saw it happen, and
maintained Guthrie had been forced off
the track by a – whisper it! – German
rider who couldn't take the corner as
fast. The Third Reich pulled out all the
stops, though. Guthrie's body was given
a military guard overnight and a special
train was laid on to take
him to the border. He
is still remembered on
the Isle of Man, where
a memorial stands at
the point at which he
retired in his final
TT. The Hawick
Museum

FERGUS ANDERSON

devotes a room to his memory and there is a statue in nearby Wilton Park, not far from a statue of Hawick's other favourite motorcycle racer, Steve Hislop (see below).

Another Scot still at his peak in his 40s was Fergus Anderson. Twice a World Grand Prix Champion, he had the distinction of being on Hitler's 'most wanted' list, although it was probably more for his work as a journalist in Hamburg than for success as a motorcycle racer. Rarely photographed without a smile on his lips (or a cigarette clamped between them), Anderson rode for Moto Guzzi. His 1953 350cc World Championship title was the first time it had been won by a non-British bike, a feat he repeated the following year. After a brief spell as Motto Guzzi's team manager – which was highly successful but rather unhappy – he went back to racing. Anderson was 47 when he died racing a works BMW on a street circuit in Belgium in 1956. He still holds the record as the oldest man to win a top-class motorcycle Grand Prix.

Bob McIntyre also lived for motor racing and died because of it. 'Bob Mac' was the most determined of racers on the track, pushing the bike to its limit – which often cost him races – but the most generous of men off it. He was a skilled mechanic, helping to design the bikes he rode. In the 1959 TT, he stripped a faulty clutch and rebuilt it in little over 12 minutes, rejoining the race to finish fifth. He is perhaps best known for his Junior and Senior Isle of Man TT titles in 1957, becoming the first man to lap the TT course at over 100mph in the process. He came close to winning the World Championship for Gilera that year until injury ended his season. He died in 1962 after crashing at Oulton Park, aged 33 years old.

BOB MCINTYRE

In 1980, Jock Taylor won the World Sidecar Championship just two years before he died in a racing accident in Finland. After two runner's up spots, he won the Isle of Man TT in 1980, breaking the lap record along the way. That season, with his Swedish passenger Benga Johannson, he finished on the podium in all seven rounds of the World Championship – winning four – to take the world title. In 1982, he hit a telegraph pole during a water-logged GP at Imatra. He survived the initial impact, but was killed as he was being removed from the wreckage when a second combination came off at the same spot.

STEVE HISLOP

It wasn't racing that killed Steve Hislop in 2003 but his preparations for life after it. 'Hizzy' – the first man to do the 'impossible' 120mph lap at the TT – died in a helicopter crash near his home town of Hawick as he trained to be a commercial pilot. Undoubtedly one of the finest riders of his era, he won 11 Isle of Man TT titles, the British 250cc Championship and was twice British Superbike Champion. Few fans of the TT will forget his epic contest with Carl Fogarty in 1992, when they went wheel-to-wheel for six laps; Hizzy on his works Norton, Foggy on a Yamaha, swapping the lead with every circuit. Hizzy won, setting a race record of 121mph, while Fogarty had the consolation of setting the outright lap record at 122.61mph.

In one poll, it was voted the greatest TT race of all time. Hislop was fearless; he rode like a demon on the track but had a reputation for acting like one off it, at least as far as his team managers were concerned. Even after he won the British Superbike series in 2002, his contract wasn't renewed, and he was sacked by his new team midway through the following season, just a few days before he died. Hizzy is still much-loved by the biking fraternity and hundreds turn out in the Borders each August for the annual Steve Hislop Memorial Run. Like Jimmy Guthrie, there is a room dedicated to his memory in the Hawick Museum and a statue in the town's Wilton Park.

A708

HOW TO USE THIS GUIDE

There are two categories of routes in this book, The Tour and The Rides. The Tour will take you on an interesting and enjoyable journey around Scotland. The Rides can be free-standing motorbike outings or can help you expand The Tour to explore the country more fully. With a bit of planning it is quite easy to link individual rides to form a longer tour or to break off from The Tour to enjoy one of The Rides. In short, it's a pick 'n' mix of routes and rides. This book has been designed for easy reference

when placed in a tank bag or carried in a pocket but, for obvious reasons, don't attempt to refer to it while moving!

Notes at the start of each route give distances to be covered and the time you should allow for the journey. The **time** is based on how long it takes to complete the route with little allowance for stops along the way. If you just want to ride your motorbike, you'll almost certainly do it faster, and if you like to hop off to clamber over castles or linger over a latte, it'll take you longer.

Each route includes step-by-step instructions. **Distances** have usually been rounded off to the nearest mile, and therefore should be regarded as a rough indication of mileage to aid navigation rather than a precise measurement! You should always err on the side of caution when estimating how far you can go before refuelling.

If you are in a remote area, and your tank is half full or less, fill up whenever you get the chance.

Where **route directions** say a road is 'signed to' a town or village, it means you will travel *towards* that place but not necessarily reach it. When the directions say 'to' a town or village, it means you continue until you have *reached* that place. All left and rights are given according to the direction of travel. **Direction of travel** indicators (see Map Key on page 33) have been numbered. Pass each marker in ascending numerical order to follow the route as set out in the directions.

We have included suggestions for things to see and do along the way, places to stay and somewhere to get a bite to eat. Our recommendations are based on the assumption that most bikers tend not to be looking for luxury accommodation or fine dining! Reasonably priced (i.e., reasonably cheap) hotels and B&Bs are the norm, and most of the places to eat in this book tend to be roadside cafés and informal bistros rather than fancy restaurants.

If you need some **music** to keep you company while you ride, you can either take a piper on the pillion like the guy in the picture, or try our playlist. On each route you will find a suggestion for some music to play on your travels, either in your headset if that's your thing, or at the start or end of the day. The tracks chosen are all by Scottish artists, or at least musicians who can claim a strong connection to Scotland. Hopefully, the suggestions might introduce you to some of the fine music being produced north of the border these days or remind you of some old favourites. This QR code links to *The Tarmap Motorcycle Guide Spotify* playlist in which you'll find the tracks featured in this guide.

We've also recommended **books** to help you find out more about the area in which you're travelling, about Scotland in general or just to help you pass the time of an evening. From 'Tartan Noir' to local folklore and classic literature, mostly by Scottish writers or writers with a connection to the country.

At the back of the book, you will find a list of telephone numbers, websites and apps which you might find useful on your trip, from weather forecasts to campsites and ferry companies.

PRONUNCIATION.

Place names in Scotland are often difficult to pronounce. When Gaelic is involved – and even when it's not – the names of many towns, villages, mountains and lochs are almost impossible to say properly without help. On page 198 we have provided guidance for some of the more challenging place names found along the way. We have not stuck to strict phonetic rules, but have tried to find a way to help you say the name in a manner which makes it sound (roughly) like it's meant to. If it's not listed, then just say it as you see it, and you won't be far wrong.

Arguably the most important skill is to master the 'voiceless velar fricative' – that's the proper name for the 'ch' found in words like 'loch' and 'Sassenach'. Think of it as the sort of sound you might make if you want to clear a fishbone that's stuck in the back of your throat. It is much the same

as the 'ch' in 'achtung'. Most English people tend to pronounce 'loch' as 'lock', but if you pronounce the 'ch' as you would in 'achtung', you're on your way to saying it as you should. Practice repeating 'Achiltibuie, Auchtermuchty and Ecclefechan' and you'll soon master it. Generally, locals like to hear you try and, however you say it, you won't come up with anything they haven't heard before!

Finally, this guide should only be used in conjunction with common sense and personal responsibility. While putting it together, all parties involved have strived for accuracy; information has been double-checked and details are as up to date as possible. Please bear in mind the date of publication and the chance that something might have changed in the interim. If you find any information that is incorrect in this guide, we sincerely hope it doesn't inconvenience you. We'd also be very grateful if you could let us know.

THE ROUTES

Although the maps have been designed to be easy to follow and the book itself has been been sized to fit into most motorcycle tank-bags, it goes without saying – but we'll say it anyway – that you should never take your eyes off the road while you are moving. Study the route carefully before departing, or pull over to check directions. Don't attempt to read maps or directions while riding a moving motorbike!

ASSYNT, SUTHERLAND

=== A9 ===	Trunk road	START	Start
=== A99 ===	A road / single track	FINISH	Finish
B851	B road / single track	🛏	Stay
————	Minor road	🍴	Eat
——●——	Railway / station	⛽	Fuel
	Woodland	★	Point of interest
		➊►	Direction of travel

Note: The maps used in this guide have varied scales.

THE SOLWAY AND CARRICK COASTS

| TWISTY | STRAIGHTER |
| SINGLE TRACK | WIDER |

DISTANCE
245 miles

ALLOW
1 day

KENNEDY'S PASS, LENDALFOOT

The southern coastline of Scotland is pretty much ignored by the majority of holidaymakers, and this in itself is a great reason to go there.

Scotland's 'secret coast' – a.k.a. The Scottish Riviera – has rolling hills, hidden beaches, quiet villages, ruined castles and very little traffic. Steeped in history – this is Robert the Bruce country – it's blessed with some really lovely roads. The main highway between Stranraer and Gretna is the A75. It's a fine road through picturesque countryside and is a veritable joy to ride… if you time it right. But time it wrong, and you'll get caught up in the Irish ferry traffic, or in rush-hour round the dreadful Dumfries by-pass. At times the A75 can feel like the M25, but the coast road a few miles to the south – which hangs like a string of bunting along the Solway Firth – takes you in the same direction with far less stress. It's longer for sure, and it's probably not a good idea if you have a ferry to catch from Cairnryan, but if you want to experience the real Dumfries and Galloway, take to the coast.

The road takes us through New Abbey, Dalbeattie and Auchencairn to Kirkcudbright, probably the most

mispronounced community in Scotland after Kirkcaldy! Then we drop down through Wigtown to arguably the prettiest harbour in the south of Scotland, the Isle of Whithorn (which isn't an island). As we head for Portpatrick, our route crosses the A716, offering the chance to turn left for a run down to Scotland's southernmost point at the Mull of Galloway. It's a 40-mile round trip but there are wonderful views to the Isle of Man, Ireland, and even Wales on a good day. From Portpatrick – another picture postcard harbour – we join the A77, which leads us through Stranraer and up to the Carrick coast. From Ballantrae to Girvan is Scotland's answer to California's Big Sur – rugged coast and a road that runs beside the shore or up above the rocks. All the while, Ailsa Craig sits out in the sea like a giant fruitcake, with the Mull of Kintyre as the backdrop. The road is great and provides plenty of

opportunities for overtaking. Okay, it's not as sexy as California, and Girvan is no Carmel, but it's still pretty good fun.

The next stretch of the A77 has a poor safety record, but we're not on it for long, turning off in time to doff our cap (or raise a middle finger, depending on your point of view) past Trump's Turnberry Hotel. The carriageway is narrower for a while through the rolling Carrick countryside and villages like Kirkmichael and Patna but, as we turn south, the countryside and the road open up. The easy curves allow the bike to get into its stride down the east side of the Galloway Forest Park, before it's back to the twisty stuff through the hills to Corsock and Crocketford. We cross the A75 to return to Dumfries on the Old Military Road, the only one in the south of Scotland. It follows a ridge back into town with the rolling Galloway farmland spread out on either side. Oh, how the soldiers must have loved marching along it on their way to subdue the Irish in the 18th century!

SOUNDTRACK

Smuggler by The McCalmans. An 18th century poem, discovered in a book called *A Pilgrimage to the Land of Burns*; Ian McCalman wrote the tune, the chorus and the final verse. It's an appropriate track for this route which travels through Ayrshire and Dumfries, the two counties most closely associated with Robert Burns.

FURTHER READING

The Grey Man by S.R. Crockett (Kennedy & Boyd, 2008). First published in 1896, this rollicking adventure is set in the south-west of Scotland during the reign of James VI. It's full of characters drawn from local folklore, including the infamous cannibal, Sawney Beane, who lived in a cave north of Ballantrae.

1 From the A75 Dumfries by-pass, turn off at the Garroch Roundabout, by the hospital, and follow signs to Cargenbridge (1 mile)

2 Turn right onto A711, signed Dalbeattie, to Beeswing (5 miles)

3 As you leave the village, turn left to New Abbey (5 miles)

4 Turn right onto A710 to Dalbeattie (18 miles)

5 As you approach Dalbeattie, turn left at crossroads onto A711 signed to Auchencairn (0.5 mile)

6 Turn left at traffic lights on A711 Auchencairn (7 miles)

7 Continue on A711 to Kirkcudbright (11 miles)

8 Turn left onto A755, signed Gatehouse of Fleet, to junction with A75 (6 miles)

9 Turn left onto A75 to roundabout at Newton Stewart (18 miles)

10 Turn left onto A714 to Wigtown (7 miles)

11 On leaving Wigtown, turn left on A714, signed to Port William (1 mile)

12 Continue ahead now on A746 to Whithorn (8 miles)

13 At far end of village, bear left onto B7004 and follow signs to Isle of Whithorn (3 miles)

14 Leave the village by the way you arrived on B7004 (1.5 miles)

15 Continue ahead onto A747 following signs for Port William (9 miles)

16 Continue on A747 to join A75 (12 miles)

17 Turn left on A75, signed Stranraer (2 miles)

18 Turn left onto B7084 and follow signs to Portpatrick (19 miles)

19 Leave Portpatrick on the road you came, following signs to Stranraer (8 miles)

20 As you head down Stranraer's Dalrymple Street, pick up signs to A77 Ayr

21 Follow A77 through Girvan to Turnberry (34 miles)

22 Turn left onto A719, signed Ayr and Maidens, to Maybole (8 miles)

23 Turn right onto B7023 Crosshill to T-junction (100 yards)

24 Turn left onto A77, signed Ayr (700 yards)

25 Turn right onto Kirkmichael Road and follow signs to Kirkmichael (3 miles)

26 Fork left as you enter the village onto Patna Road to Patna (5 miles)

27 Turn right onto A713, signed Castle Douglas, passing through St John's Town of Dalry to Ken Bridge Hotel (26 miles)

28 Turn left onto A712 to Crocketford (14 miles)

29 Turn right on A75 Stranraer (150 yards)

30 Turn left (unsigned) onto unclassified road to T-junction (2 miles)

31 Turn left and follow the Old Military Road back to Dumfries (8 miles)

WHAT TO SEE

Let's face it, wouldn't we all occasionally like to cut out our partner's heart and put it in a box? Lady Devorgilla of Galloway did just that back in 1273 (he was dead at the time) and she carried the heart with her for the rest of her life. When she and the box were buried together at the new abbey, the monks were so touched that they called the building 'Sweetheart Abbey' (DG2 8BU). The village is still called New Abbey; you pass the 'old' abbey at Dundrennan a few miles further on.

Galloway Tanks (DG8 8AB) at Garlieston, Whithorn, have tanks, personnel carriers and 4x4s to drive and plenty of land to drive them on. Book in advance.

The Electric Brae is a couple of miles off our route between Culzean Castle and Maybole. It's an optical illusion in which your bike will appear to freewheel uphill.

LOOK OUT FOR

Belted Galloways – big black cows with a white waistband. They're locals.

WHERE TO STAY

The Steam Packet Inn (DG8 8LL), Isle of Whithorn, offers great food and friendly service. The setting is a delight as well.

Trump Turnberry Hotel. No, please. Don't. Just don't!

The Clachan Inn, St John's Town of Dalry (DG7 3UW). Good food, great atmosphere. Single rooms available.

WHERE TO EAT

The Crown Hotel (DG9 8SX) in Portpatrick is a popular eating place for bikers (and others). It does excellent crab sandwiches.

Dowhill Country Fayre (KA26 9JP) between Girvan and Turnberry offers good filling food at reasonable prices.

ROUTE 02
AROUND THE MERRICK

TWISTY	STRAIGHTER	**DISTANCE**	167 miles
SINGLE TRACK	WIDER	**ALLOW**	5 hours

THE DALVEEN PASS

This route starts close to the M74 – the motorway between Glasgow and the English border – before twisting its way over to the coast and back, and circling the Merrick, southern Scotland's highest hill. It's a blast from start to finish – easy to access and a joy to ride.

The village of Abington, close to J13 on the M74, makes a good starting point, and the local shop makes great coffee. To begin, it's south on the 'service road' beside the motorway before turning off through Elvanfoot and down the magnificent Dalveen Pass. With a good surface, sympathetic cambers and reassuring lines of sight, it's easy to see why it's popular with local bikers. A right turn in Thornhill takes you to Moniaive, with a stirring little short-cut through Tynron and over Dunreggan Brae, a 1:4 gradient single track with branches hanging so low you may have to duck. From Moniaive, it's over the high ground to St John's Town of Dalry (more commonly referred to as Dalry), before turning left for New Galloway. You can open the throttle again on the Queen's Way to Newton Stewart, watching out for Irish bikers letting off steam after getting off the ferry at Stranraer. As you

pass Clatteringshaws Loch, the Merrick is over to your right, about nine miles as the crow flies.

Then we turn right for Girvan. It's a decent road over the moor to Barrhill before it gets a bit twisty and bumpy – with fewer overtaking opportunities – until you start descending towards the Firth of Clyde at Girvan, with Ailsa Craig sitting reassuringly offshore. At the north end of the town, the fun restarts as you turn right for Barr, climbing, twisting and turning through a strangely attractive wind farm before dropping down into the Stinchar valley. The road into Barr is known locally as 'The Screws' – it's not long, but it's certainly invigorating and you may decide to go back to the top and do it again. I did. From Barr, we follow the River Stinchar

upstream then over the Nick o' the Balloch, riding high on the valley side as you pass between hills and into the Galloway Forest Park. The landscape is dominated by commercial forestry and moorland for much of the way to Straiton – single track, but well surfaced and demanding. It's a brilliant ride and, at times, it feels a bit like you're in a tumble dryer. With the possibility that you might meet a timber truck at any moment, it's an adrenaline-filled but rip-roaring few miles.

Things straighten out from the old mining village of Dalmellington to New Cumnock where we join the A76, all long straights and sweeping curves to Sanquhar and beyond. Just after Mennock, we turn into the

Mennock Pass to follow the valley floor up to Scotland's highest village at Wanlockhead. Then a final canter over the moorland through Leadhills and back to the start. Wunderbar! Utterly wunderbar!

SOUNDTRACK

Cumbia Celtica by Salsa Celtica, Scotland's own hard-rocking, kilt-swinging, dance floor-filling Celtic salsa band.

FURTHER READING

Built by Nobles of Girvan by Sam Henderson and Peter Drummond (The History Press, 2010). The Firth of Clyde used to have dozens of small boatyards along its banks. Nobles, in Girvan harbour, is a rare survivor.

HEADING FOR STRAITON

WHAT TO SEE

The Duke of Buccleuch owns three stately homes, but only one – **Drumlanrig** (DG3 4AQ) – has a **Cycle Museum** complete with a replica of Kirkpatrick Macmillan's first bicycle. Note that you can't visit the museum unless you buy a ticket to the castle. Near Sanquhar, **Crawick Multiverse** (DG4 6ET) is an old open-cast coal mine that has been converted into a 55-acre outdoor art space. Extraordinary!

The **Museum of Lead Mining** (ML12 6UT) in Wanlockhead offers the chance to enter a genuine mine shaft.

LOOK OUT FOR

The world's oldest post office in Sanquhar's High Street (DG4 6DJ). It began as a staging post for mail carriages in 1712 and has been open on the same site ever since.

People in the burn south of Wanlockhead. They're panning for gold. These here hills have more than lowly lead in them.

WHERE TO STAY

The **Ken Bridge Hotel** (DG7 3PR) in New Galloway is an old coaching inn sitting on the banks of the river. Informal and convenient, it also has camping pitches. To wake up to views of Aisla Craig, try the **Woodland Bay** (KA26 0HP), just south of Girvan.

WHERE TO EAT

For a good wholesome refuelling stop, you won't find better than **The Smithy café** (DG7 3RN) in New Galloway, where you'll receive a warm welcome, good food and sensible prices. **Brew Ha Ha** (DG8 6BW) on Newton Stewart's main street is a wee café with a big garden.

The **Harbour Café** (KA26 9AG) in Girvan does a mean fish & chips – find the harbour and you've found the café. If it's open, **Barr Stores** (KA26 9TU) is community owned and ever-so hospitable. "Do you serve soup?" was the question. "Well, if you want to choose a tin off the shelves, I can heat it up for you." How obliging is that?

1 The village of Abington is on the A702, a mile south of the service station at J13 on the M74. With the hotel on your right, head south on the A702 (5 miles)

2 Turn right on A702, passing under the motorway, and follow signs to Thornhill (18 miles)

3 At Thornhill 30mph signs, turn right on A702, signed Moniaive (3 miles)

4 Bear right to T-junction at Tynron war memorial (2 miles)

5 Turn right (unsigned) to Moniaive (2 miles)

6 Turn right into the village to the Craigdarroch Arms Hotel (150 yards)

7 Turn left on A702 to Dalry (13 miles)

8 At the T-junction, turn left onto A713, signed Castle Douglas, to the Ken Bridge Hotel (3 miles)

9 Turn right over a bridge onto A712 into New Galloway (1 mile)

10 Take second turning on the right, on A712 signed Newton Stewart (17 miles)

11 Just before the T-junction, turn right onto B7079 to Newton Stewart (1 mile)

12 After crossing the River Cree, turn right onto A714 to Girvan (29 miles)

13 Cross the roundabout onto A77 into Girvan, following signs to Ayr to lead through the town

14 After passing under a railway bridge, cross the roundabout onto B734 and follow signs to Barr (7 miles) NB: Turn sharp right in Old Dailly after 2 miles, and bear left almost 1 mile later.

15 In Barr, turn left into Glenginnet Road to T-junction (4 miles)

16 Turn right to T-junction (4 miles)

17 Turn left to Straiton (12 miles)

18 In the main street, turn right onto B741, signed Dalmellington to T-junction (6 miles)

19 Turn right onto A713 to Dalmellington, (700 yards)

20 After the petrol station, turn left onto B741 to New Cumnock (11 miles)

21 Turn right onto A76, signed Sanquhar, continuing to Mennock (13 miles)

22 Turn left onto B797 to Wanlockhead, Leadhills and Abington (15 miles)

ROUTE 03
RIDING THE MARCHES

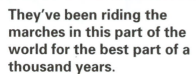

| TWISTY | STRAIGHTER |
| SINGLE TRACK | WIDER |

DISTANCE
180 miles

ALLOW
6 hours

LIDDESDALE

They've been riding the marches in this part of the world for the best part of a thousand years.

Since the 12th century, young men of the burghs have regularly checked the boundaries ('marches') of the common land to make sure their neighbours haven't encroached. The tradition still continues in towns across the south of Scotland in annual festivals, known as 'Common Ridings'. This route rides the biggest 'march' of them all – the border between Scotland and England, from the Solway Firth to the North Sea coast. When the border between Scotland and England was established in the 13th century, some areas remained in dispute. These 'debatable lands' were ungoverned, untamed and lawless territories where tribal thugs, called reivers (from the Old Scots word for 'robber') regarded anyone with a different surname as fair game. Reivers robbed, murdered, kidnapped and generally terrorised the populations on behalf of their family chief.

The hills and valleys along the south of Scotland are a lot safer these days and make for terrific motorcycling country. Quiet, curving roads pick their way between the rolling hills, eventually giving way to the fast, fertile plains

of Berwickshire as you draw near the east coast. This route occasionally dips into England, although as you criss-cross the border, you'll see little difference between the two nations. The village of Newcastleton (known locally as Copshaw Holm) is long and thin, but geometrically impressive. It's a jinking run through the Border hills to Jedburgh, arriving by the abbey and leaving by the rugby ground. After a few miles with the throttle open, we're back in the hills to Morebattle, Yetholm and over the border. The roads in Northumberland carry us through peaceful farmland that was fought over for centuries. Berwick, or Berwick-upon-Tweed to give it the

full title, is a robustly fortified town that passed between Scottish and English hands at regular intervals. Now, although currently English, it keeps its options open by allowing its football team, Berwick Rangers, to play in the Scottish leagues. We return through the long, straight Berwickshire roads to Chirnside, Duns and Greelaw – good roads but with plenty of bends to keep us alert. After a visit to another of the ruined Border Abbeys, at Dryburgh, we're crossing to Selkirk, for the delicious run down the A7. It has to rank as one of finest trunk roads in Scotland and it leads over the hills to Hawick and through the valleys to Canonbie, Longtown and home.

SOUNDTRACK

The Rolling Hills of the Borders by Matt McGinn. An old style troubadour and raconteur, he wrote hundreds of songs, many of which have become folk standards.

FURTHER READING

The Debatable Land: The Lost World Between Scotland and England by Graham Robb (Picador, 2018). A history of the Borders, the reivers and their place in the world. Written with the flair of a novelist.

↓ **1** From the roundabout at the Gretna Gateway Outlet Village (DG16 5GG), head south (leaving the petrol station to your right)

↑ **2** Follow the B7076 across the motorway towards Longtown to T-junction (4 miles)

↰ **3** Turn left onto A7, signed Galashiels (3 miles)

↦ **4** Turn right to Canonbie and follows signs to Newcastleton (12 miles)

↑ **5** Continue on B6357 to cross a bridge (1.5 miles)

↦ **6** Turn right on B6357 and follow signs to Bonchester Bridge (16 miles)

↦ **7** Turn right on B6357 and follow signs to Jedburgh (7 miles)

↑ **8** Follow A68 through Jedburgh to Bonjedward (2 miles)

↦ **9** Turn right for 350 yards, then right again onto A698, signed Kelso (4 miles)

↦ **10** Turn right onto B6401 to Morebattle and on to Town Yetholm (9 miles)

↦ **11** Turn right onto B6352, signed Wooler, to crossroads (4 miles)

↑ **12** Cross over onto unclassified road to Cornhill (4 miles)

↱ **13** Turn right onto A698 to roundabout (400 yards)

↻ **14** Continue ahead on A698 and follow signs to Berwick-upon-Tweed (13 miles)

↰ **15** In centre of town, turn left, passing the railway station, and cross the railway (0.5 mile)

↰ **16** Bear right for Edinburgh to roundabout by Morrison's supermarket (1 mile)

↰ **17** Turn left onto A1 (0.5 mile)

↦ **18** Turn right onto A6105 to Duns (14 miles)

↑ **19** Continue on A6105, through Greenlaw, to Earlston (18 miles)

↰ **20** Turn left (after traffic lights) onto B6356 to T-junction (2.5 miles)

↱ **21** Turn right, then left, signed Bemersyde, to T-junction (3.5 miles)

↱ **22** Turn right onto B6404 for St Boswells (2 miles)

↰ **23** Turn left onto A68 for 400 yards, then turn right onto A699, signed Selkirk, to T-junction (8 miles)

↰ **24** Turn left on A7, through Hawick & Langholm towards Longtown (44 miles)

↦ **25** Just before Longtown, turn right onto A6071 to Gretna (4 miles)

WHAT TO SEE

Flodden Field (TD12 4SS) near Cornhill, where the largest Scottish army ever to invade England suffered a disastrous defeat in 1513. **Chain Bridge Honey Farm** (TD15 2XT) near Horncliffe, signed to the left eight miles after direction No.14 above. There's a fine collection of old vehicles and the café is in a double-decker bus. Nearby is the chain bridge itself, the **Union Bridge** (TD15 1XQ) linking Scotland to England. It's probably the finest of all the border crossing points.

LOOK OUT FOR

The Border abbeys. These 12th century abbeys were built in lands where peace was rare, and they suffered as a result. The ruins are impressive and this route passes two of them: Jedburgh and Dryburgh.

WHERE TO STAY

The Plough Hotel (TD5 8PF) in Yetholm offers great accommodation in a quiet village. Good food in the bar means you don't have to go out in the evening either!

Wiltonburn Farm B&B (TD9 7LL), just south of Hawick. Lovely house, in a lovely setting, with lovely rooms. In short? Lovely.

WHERE TO EAT

Brown Sugar Coffee Shop (TD8 6AJ) in Jedburgh has been there for ever and the food is still great. In Berwick, **Sinners Café** (TD15 1DR) is tucked away in Sidey Court, just off the main street (opposite Iceland).

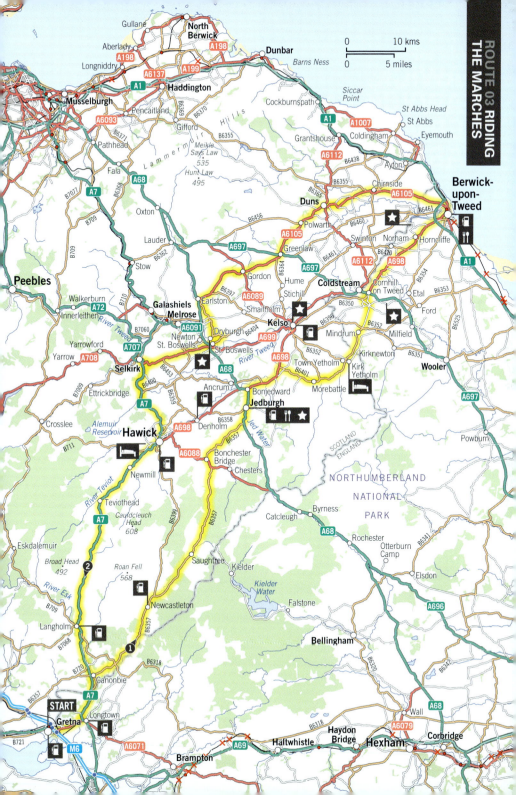

Gullane

North
Berwick

Aberlady

A198

Dunbar

Longniddry

Barns Ness

A198

A6137

A199

A1

Haddington

Musselburgh

Pencaitland

*Siccar
Point*

Cockburnspath

B6370

A1007

St Abbs Head

A6093

Gifford

B6369

B6355

A1

St Abbs

Pathhead

B6371

Grantshouse

Coldingham

Eyemouth

Fala

Lammermuir

B6355

A6112

B6438

Ayton

Oxton

A68

*Meikle
Says Law
535*

B6365

B6355

Chirnside

A7

B6368

Hills

B6456

B6461

A6105

B6461

Berwick-
upon-
Tweed

B709

*Hunt Law
495*

Duns

Lauder

A697

Polwarth

B6460

Norham

Horncliffe

Peebles

B710

Stow

B6362

Greenlaw

A6105

Swinton

B6470

A1

Walkerburn

A72

Gordon

B6364

A697

A6112

A698

B6354

Innerleithen

B7060

A6089

B6397

Hume
Stichill

Coldstream

Cornhill
on Tweed

Etal

B6353

Galashiels
Melrose

Earlston

Smailholm

B6350

Ford

River Tweed

A6091

B6404

Dryburgh

B6396

Mindrum

Milfield

Yarrowford

Newton
St. Boswells

A699

Kelso

B6352

Yarrow

A707

St. Boswells

River Tweed

A698

Kirknewton

B6351

A708

Selkirk

B6433

B6400

B6359

Ancrum

A68

Bonjedward

Town Yetholm

Kirk
Yetholm

Wooler

Crosslee

B6359

A698

Jedburgh

B6401

Morebattle

A697

Ettrickbridge

A7

Denholm

B6358

Powburn

*Alemuir
Reservoir*

B711

Hawick

A698

Jed Water

SCOTLAND
ENGLAND

A6088

Bonchester
Bridge

B709

Newmill

Chesters

NORTHUMBERLAND

River Teviot

B6399

B6357

Teviothead

NATIONAL

A7

*Cauldcleuch
Head
608*

Catcleugh

Byrness

PARK

Eskdalemuir

*Broad Head
492*

②

*Roan Fell
568*

Saughtree

Kielder

A68

Rochester

Otterburn
Camp

Elsdon

A696

River Esk

B709

Newcastleton

B6357

*Kielder
Water*

Falstone

Langholm

B7068

B6357

①

Bellingham

B6320

B6342

B220

Canonbie

B6318

A7

START

Longtown

Gretna

Wall

A68

B721

M6

A6071

B6318

A6079

Hexham

Corbridge

Brampton

A69

Haltwhistle

Haydon
Bridge

B6357

0   10 kms
0   5 miles

HAWICK, DAWYCK AND HERMITAGE CASTLE

TWISTY ▬▬ **STRAIGHTER**	**DISTANCE** 138 miles
SINGLE TRACK ▬▬ **WIDER**	**ALLOW** 4 hours

TALLA RESERVOIR

Hawick is a fine old Borders town, famous for turning out some of the best Scottish rugby players, some of the best Scottish knitwear and some of the best Scottish motorcycle racers.

Hawick sits on the A7 and we follow that road to Selkirk, before turning west through the former mill communities of Walkerburn and Innerleithen. It's a delightful if sometimes busy road, but there's an equally lovely – and quieter – alternative on the other side of the river, through Traquair and Cardrona. Both bring us to the bustling market town of Peebles, a royal burgh since the 12th century and apparently thriving in the 21st. We follow the Tweed upriver for the next 20 miles, passing the impressive Neidpath Castle before turning off for a leafy road past the Royal Botanical Garden's arbitorum at Dawyck and on, through Drumelzier, to the brilliant A701. This road will take you quickly and enjoyably to Moffat if you let it, but we're turning off at Tweedsmuir, after running beside an old railway line built for the sole purpose of getting men and material to the construction site for the Talla Reservoir. When they finished the dam, they closed the railway! Talla was constructed in 1899 when public buildings were built with architectural integrity – even the overflow is a little Victorian treasure. Water from Talla flows by gravity alone to taps in Edinburgh. At the head of the reservoir the road climbs steeply uphill without passing places, so check nothing is coming down before you head up.

Your fairing will get a shaking as you make for Megget Reservoir, and you share the narrow road with sheep. The Megget dam was built in the 1980s and is a relatively drab affair, although it is said to be the largest earth dam in Scotland. We pass the picturesque old AA box at Cappercleuch as we turn north onto the wider Selkirk road for a

few miles. Then it's back onto single track (although well-surfaced this time) to Tushielaw and up the steep-sided Rankle Glen to Alemoor Reservoir. The A7 is arguably the best motorcycling highway between Scotland and England; the route is picturesque without being restrictive, and it's a joyful run down towards Langholm. Now hairpin bends help us up back into hills, past the monument to the poet Hugh MacDiarmid. The passage over the moors is pretty isolated – it's fairly unusual to feel this alone in the south of Scotland. Next is a brief detour to Hermitage Castle, the bleak keep that guards the even bleaker landscape like the Grim Reaper himself. Steeped in both history and blood, the owner was once boiled to death in lead from the castle roof. Fine architecture speaks to the beholder and Hermitage seems to be telling the world to "**** off", so we will – back to Hawick, on an exhilarating road more or less following the trackbed of the famous (but long since closed) Waverley Line.

SOUNDTRACK

 And We Ride by Scocha, pronounced Scotia. They're folk 'n' rollers from Hawick.

FURTHER READING

 Anything by Walter Scott, although his books are heavy going by today's standard. You could instead seek out a film or TV version of *Ivanhoe*. (Or not.)

HERMITAGE CASTLE

1 Leave Hawick on the A7 to Selkirk's Market Place (11 miles)

2 As A7 turns sharp right, go straight ahead into West Port, go down the hill to pick up signs to Peebles A707 (A72) (21 miles)

3 In Peebles High Street, turn right in front of the church on A72, signed Glasgow (4 miles)

4 Turn left onto B712 to Stobo & Drumelzier to T-junction (7 miles)

5 Turn left onto A701, signed Moffat (7 miles)

6 Turn left into unclassified road to Talla, passing two reservoirs to T-junction (12 miles)

7 Turn left onto A707, signed Selkirk, to crossroads at The Gordon Arms (4 miles)

8 Turn right onto B709, signed Langholm, to T-junction (6 miles)

9 Turn right following B709, signed Langholm, to Tushielaw Inn (0.5 mile)

10 Turn left onto B711, signed Hawick, to T-junction (14 miles)

11 Turn right onto A7, signed Langholm, to bridge with traffic lights (21 miles)

12 500 yards beyond the bridge, turn left onto unclassified road to Newcastleton (9 miles)

13 Turn left onto South Hermitage Street, following the road out of the village to road junction for Hermitage Castle (5 miles)

14 Turn left onto unclassified road to Hermitage Castle (1 mile)

15 Return to B6399 and turn left to Hawick (16 miles)

WHAT TO SEE

Hermitage Castle (TD9 0LU). Now that's a real castle! It was at the centre of the Anglo-Scottish border struggles for over 400 years, guarding what has been described as "the bloodiest valley in Britain". **The Hawick Museum** (TD9 7JL) in Wilton Lodge has rooms dedicated to motorcycling legends Jimmy Guthrie and Steve Hislop. There are also statues of the great men in nearby Wilton Park.

LOOK OUT FOR

The 19th century cast-iron 'pissoir' in **Walkerburn** (EH43 6AG), close to the war memorial. One of the country's more practical listed buildings, it's still in use... and free!

WHERE TO STAY

The Tushielaw Inn (TD7 5HT) feels like it's miles from anywhere – and it is – but it has bags of character, very reasonable prices and a refreshing lack of formality. After being closed for several years, it's good to see the old place back in action!

WHERE TO EAT

The **Copshaw Kitchen** (TD9 0RB), North Hermitage Street, Newcastleton. Friendly and welcoming eatery serving good, wholesome food in a village that the locals call Copshaw Holm.

Nashy's Coffee House (EH45 9HX) in Cardrona's atmospheric old station building is a terrific café with a menu that will please any biker. This is the place to try a haggis bagel.

Eddleston

A701

A702

A721

Blyth Bridge

A703

Glentress Forest

Peebles

Glentress

Cardrona

B709

Walkerburn

A72

Lauder

B6362

Stow

B710

Galashiels

Skirling

B7016

Biggar

Broughton

Stobo

Dawyck

B712

A72

Drumelzier

Stob Law 786

Innerleithen

Traquair

B7062

River Tweed

B7060

Melrose

Culter Fell 748

2

A701

Dollar Law 817

B709

Yarrow

Yarrow Feus

A707

A7

A708

Yarrowford

Selkirk

A699

B6453

B6400

Ashkirk

B6359

Tweedsmuir

Cappercleuch

St Mary's Loch

Kirkhope

Ettrickbridge

A7

Talla Reservoir

Megget Reservoir

Lochcraig Head 800

B7009

Crosslee

Alemuir Reservoir

1

Fruid Reservoir

Hart Fell 808

Ettrick Valley

Ettrick

B709

Ettrick Water

B711

Craik Forest

3

Burnfoot

Roberton

START

Hawick

A698

Moffat

A74(M)

A708

Craik

River Teviot

Newmill

Teviothead

A7

Cauldcleuch Head 608

5

B6399

Beattock

Eskdalemuir Forest

A701

B7020

Wamphray

Eskdalemuir

B723

Broad Head 492

4

Roan Fell 568

Forest of Ae

Boreland

River Esk

B709

Newcastleton

B6357

SCOTLAND ENGLAND

Lochmaben

Lockerbie

A709

A74(M)

B7068

Langholm

A7

B6357

B6318

B7020

B7076

A75

B725

B720

Canonbie

B6357

0   10 kms
0   5 miles

ROUTE 05
MOFFAT AND SELKIRK

TWISTY	STRAIGHTER
SINGLE TRACK	WIDER

DISTANCE
83 miles

ALLOW
2.5 hours

In the middle of Selkirk the local people have erected a statue to one of Britain's foremost explorers – the heroic, Selkirk-born, died-in-action, Africa-exploring Mungo Park. In Moffat, they've put up a statue of a sheep! (Okay, it's a ram but that's still a sheep.)

Between the two you'll find some of the best motorcycling roads in the country, certainly in lowland Scotland. The most direct route between the towns is the wonderful A708, a real biker's classic. It has three distinct sections – to the south it's a convoluted, helter-skelter of a road beside the Moffat Water; the middle section is a wide, dramatic hillscape past St Mary's Loch; and it's an intimate, tree-lined river valley at the Selkirk end. Delightful from start to finish. There's a good photo opportunity at the old AA box at Cappercleuch by St Mary's Loch, one of only 19 such boxes to survive.

Moffat has always been welcoming weary travellers. Although the town was built on the back of the wool trade (hence the statue of the ram), it was an important staging post between Glasgow, Edinburgh and England.

MOFFAT WATER

The main street is lined with hotels dating back to the days of coaches and horses – each with an arch leading to a stable yard behind. Moffat enjoyed a resurgence as a spa town in the 18th and 19th centuries, when people came to 'take the waters'. It's still a busy little place, and a popular stop-off point for people travelling on the nearby M7 and for bikers enjoying the many brilliant roads that seem to converge on the town. Although the A708 between Moffat and Selkirk is the stellar road in this little circuit, the others also deserve our appreciation. From Selkirk the route follows the picturesque Ettrick

Valley through the hills to Eskdalemuir. From there it's an open throttle along the wide highway to Boreland – a mixture of perfect surface and alarming potholes, but a blast nonetheless. Look out for pony carriages from the Chariots of Fire Driving Centre in Boreland, where they do great work with people with disabilities, including driving their carriages along the main road. From Boreland, the road surface is pretty dreadful for much of the way back to Moffat, as we head 'over the Windshiels' to Wamphray (single track with timber lorries) and up the old Glasgow-Carlisle coach road into Moffat. In a word? Brilliantfun!

SOUNDTRACK

Craigieburn Wood by Emily Smith (words by Robert Burns). The woods are a couple of miles from Moffat on the A708, on the bend with traffic lights.

FURTHER READING

The Hidden Ways: Scotland's Forgotten Roads by Alistair Moffat (Canongate, 2017)

↑ **1** In the centre of Moffat, put the ram statue on your right, and head downhill, leaving Marchbanks Bakery to your right

↰ **2** Bear left onto the A708 to Selkirk (33 miles)

↱ **3** Turn right at T-junction onto A707 (300 yards)

↦ **4** After crossing the river, take the first right into Ettrick Road (300 yards)

↑ **5** Follow Ettrick Road, soon the B7009/B709 to Eskdalemuir (30 miles)

↦ **6** At the church, turn right onto B723 to Boreland (7 miles)

↦ **7** Soon after the village, turn right, signed Moffat, to T-junction (5 miles). *(If you prefer the avoid the narrow, potholed, final section to Moffat, don't turn right after Boreland, but continue on the B723 (ignoring the left turn to Lockerbie) until the tall chimney of Steven's Croft power station is on your right. Turn left, then right onto the 'service road' towards Beattock, until you pick up signs to Moffat. It's longer but it's a faster road!)*

↱ **8** Turn right and follow the road to T-junction in Moffat (6 miles)

↰ **9** Turn left to return to the town centre (0.5 mile)

WHAT TO SEE

The **Samye Ling Tibetan Buddhist monastery** (DG13 0QL) in Eskdalemuir is an incongruous sight in the Scottish hills. The monastery is open to visitors, although when I last called in, a notice in the window said the café was "Closed for lunch"! Or visit **John Louden McAdam's grave** (DG10 9EH) in the cemetery at the bottom of Moffat's High Street. He lived for a while in Dumcrieff House just outside the town. The graveyard is two storey; when they ran out of space in 1747, they covered the graves in four feet of soil and started again.

LOOK OUT FOR

The **ears on the ram statue** in Moffat. (You won't see them – the statue was cast before anyone noticed the ram would be deaf.)

There's a **replica Spitfire** parked in the garden of a bungalow in The Glebe in Moffat (DG10 9ER), opposite the town's Station Park. The garden is private land, but you can get a decent view from the pavement.

The Ettrick Shepherd. On the hillside by the Glen Café by St Mary's Loch (TD7 5LH) is a white statue of James Hogg, a shepherd and poet who became a famous literary figure in the 19th century. The information boards nearby tell the story.

WHERE TO STAY

Top honours have to go to the **Buccleuch Arms Hotel** (DG10 9ET) in Moffat. It gets special mention because of the sheer commitment the team put into promoting motorcycling in Scotland and looking after bikers – and others – who stay there. Run by bikers and very biker friendly, it's an example to others. Good food and accommodation as well.

Nether Boreland B&B (DG11 2LL) is an old coaching inn which is now part of an equestrian centre, specialising in carriage driving. Delightfully informal, they'll put your bike under cover on request, and supply an evening meal if given advance warning. The chance to drive a pony and carriage is also on offer.

WHERE TO EAT

For a quick bite, the **Glen Café** (TD7 5LH) is a popular stop at Tibbie Shiels, by the southern end of St Mary's Loch. The craic is good on a sunny weekend. There are several cafés in Moffat – I've a soft spot for **Café Ariete** (DG10 9HF) on the main street, and you won't find a better coffee than you get at **Brodies** (DG10 9HF). At the Selkirk end, make for **The Waterwheel** (TD7 5LU) at Philiphaugh.

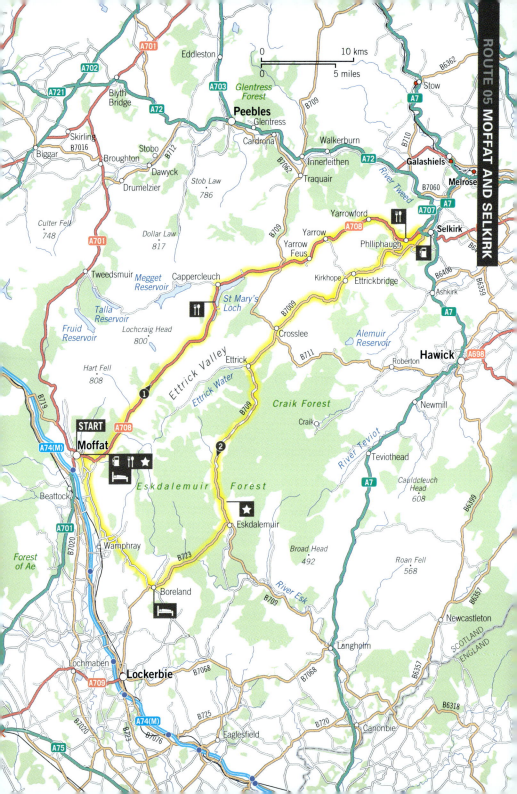

KINTYRE

| TWISTY | STRAIGHTER | DISTANCE 201 miles |
| SINGLE TRACK | WIDER | ALLOW 1 day |

Back in the days when the Vikings were pushing their weight around, Magnus Barelegs (so called because he wore an early form of kilt) persuaded King Malcolm III of Scotland to let him have control of any land that he could take his boat round.

WEST LOCH TARBERT

So he sailed along the Kintyre peninsula before making the crew haul his longship overland across Tarbert to West Tarbert while he was at the helm, thereby completing the circuit and claiming the prize. In the 11th century, Kintyre wasn't the quiet backwater it is today. Whatever else has happened in the area over the past 1,000 years, the roads have certainly improved. From start to finish they're either wide and encouraging or narrow and interesting. It's quite possible to do Kintyre in a day, but the place really rewards those who stay longer. These days it's being marketed as the 'Argyll 190' – roughly the distance travelled on a round trip from Inveraray.

The route itself is straightforward, the difficult decision being how to get to Inveraray in the first place. Most people head up the A83, through Glen Croe from Arrochar and over the Rest and Be Thankful. It's a gratifying run; fast and

flowing all the way to the traffic lights on the bridge by Inveraray Castle. An alternative route – and the one we're taking – goes via Dunoon to enjoy the Cowal Peninsula before heading over to Kintyre. It's every bit as thrilling and two short ferry hops only add to the sense of adventure. So here's our 'Argyll 201'. Highlights include the single track road across from Dunoon to the top of Loch Striven – twisting and undulating along a race-track-smooth surface before an exhilarating climb up the hillside and down to Ormidale. Then it's up again to overlook the Kyles of Bute – don't pass the viewpoint without stopping – and on to the ferry at Portavadie. It docks in Tarbert, where Kintyre almost becomes an island, and where we join the A83 from Arrochar. After climbing above the western shore, with glimpses of the water to the west, the view opens and the road drops to sea level. Now it runs

along beside the beach or is separated from the sea only by rocks. The views out to Gigha and Islay are stunning and the roads are straight, open, empty and fast. Twenty miles later, we turn inland to Campbeltown.

You can't come this far without going the extra mile or so to Southend, and on (another seven) to the end of the public road from where you can walk down to the lighthouse. The thought of the walk back up might put you off the idea but, if you don't go to the lighthouse, you haven't really been to 'The Mull of Kintyre' ('Mull' is from the old Norse word for 'headland'). We set off north from Campbeltown along the east side of Kintyre, beside the Firth of Clyde, with views to Ailsa Craig, the Ayrshire coast and Arran. It's single track beyond Carradale, rising and falling with some unexpected bends and uninterrupted

views, until we rejoin the A83 for Tarbert. Now we're on faster roads again, up the side of Loch Fyne, past the southern end of the Crinan Canal at Ardrishaig, through Lochgilphead and onto Inveraray and Arrochar. There you are! A trip to the Mull of Kintyre and I didn't mention Paul McCartney once. (Oh, bugger!)

SOUNDTRACK

Band on the Run by Wings (because it's better than *Mull of Kintyre*)

FURTHER READING

Whisky From Small Glasses by Denzil Meyrick (Polygon, 2014) is the first in his series of DCI Daley crime thrillers. Meyrick was raised in Kintyre and, as well as being a former policeman, once managed a distillery in Campbeltown.

SKIPNESS

WHAT TO SEE

A film in **Campbeltown's Picture House** (PA28 6BU). It's one of the oldest cinemas in the country and an art nouveau masterpiece, sympathetically refurbished in 2017. Never mind what's showing, go see the cinema!

St Columba's Footprints at Southend (PA28 6RW). There are two footprints carved in stone near the shore where it's said St Columba stepped ashore from Ireland in 563. One is probably not his footprint (although it's certainly ancient) while the other is definitely not. It was carved by a local stonemason in 1856 as a way of drumming up more interest for visitors. He also carved the date when he thought Columba came ashore, but he got it wrong. Nearby are **St Columba's Well** and the **Keil Caves.**

Check the tides before walking out to **Davaar** (PA28 6SL), the island at the mouth of Campbeltown Loch. At low water, it takes about 40 minutes to cross the shingle causeway where you'll find caves, one of which features Archibald MacKinnon's famous 1887 crucifixion painting on the wall. Don't cross without taking local advice about the tides – you'll have several lonely hours to admire the painting if you get it wrong!

LOOK OUT FOR

Mist rolling in from the sea.

WHERE TO STAY

The Argyll Hotel (PA28 6QE) at Bellochantuy on the west coast. Just feet from the sea, good food, nice rooms and decent rates. If it's not raining and you half close your eyes, it's quite like Malibu!

The Grammar Lodge Guesthouse (PA28 6AU) in Campbeltown is a bit more expensive but you can't fault the place. Top notch.

WHERE TO EAT

Muneroy Tearoom and Store at Southend (PA28 6RW). It's almost in Antrim! They deserve support just for trading this far away from everywhere. It's quirky, reliable and very welcome at the end of a long ride south.

Skipness Seafood Cabin (PA29 6XU). A lovely informal experience in an unexpected setting. Superb food eaten under an awning if it's raining, in the open air if it's not. A castle on one side, Arran on the other and delicious seafood in front of you.

Three Villages Café and Pit Stop Diner in Arrochar (G83 7AB). Community-run café complete with en-suite post office. Food is good and the prices spot on.

HEADING FOR THE LIGHTHOUSE, MULL OF KINTYRE

BELLOCHANTUY

1 From Western Ferries terminal in Gourock (PA19 1BA) cross to Dunoon. If you have time, buy your tickets before boarding from Paul's Food and Wine in Shore Street (PA19 1RB). It's about half the price of buying them on the boat.

2 From the ferry at Hunters Quay (Dunoon), turn right to a T-junction (2 miles)

3 Turn right, signed Glasgow (1.5 miles)

4 Turn left onto B836, signed Colintraive (11 miles)

5 Turn right onto A886, signed Strachur (1.3 miles)

6 Turn left onto A8003 and follow signs to Portavadie Marina, then picking up signs to Tarbert Ferry (12 miles)

7 Take the ferry

8 From the slipway, follow road to T-junction (0.5 mile)

9 Turn left onto A83 to Campbeltown (37 miles)

10 Turn left at T-junction into Main Street (100 yards)

11 Turn right on roundabout along the seafront (250 yards)

12 Turn right on mini-roundabout (50 yards)

13 Bear left onto Kilkerran Road and continue past Davaar Island down to Southend (14 miles) *(Go right at the first T junction after 12 miles, and left at the second, to reach Southend)*

14 Follow the road past St Columba's Chapel before turning back inland (3 miles)

15 Turn left to Mull of Kintyre Lighthouse (6 miles)

16 Return to T-junction (6 miles)

17 Turn left and follow signs to Campbeltown (10 miles)

18 In Campbeltown, put the harbour on your right-hand side

19 Turn right into The Esplanade to T-junction (500 yards)

20 Turn right onto B842 (Carradale) and follow it to T-junction (32 miles)

21 Turn right on A83 to Arrochar (65 miles) (or return via ferries to Gourock)

SOUTH LANARKSHIRE

TWISTY	STRAIGHTER
SINGLE TRACK	WIDER

DISTANCE
110 miles

ALLOW
3 hours

HOLEHOUSE LINN, NEAR MOFFAT

Biggar is a busy wee market town straddling the main road from Edinburgh to the south-west, a shortcut from the capital to the M74/M6 motorway.

Its motto? "Londinium magnum est sed Biggar Biggar est" – Latin for "London's big, but Biggar's Biggar". The main street is lined with independent shops and cafés and, if it wasn't for the traffic thundering through the middle of town, it would be idyllic. As we leave Biggar, heading north, the enjoyment begins immediately, the road lifting and turning through the hills over to Carnwath. Here we join the old highway from Edinburgh to Ayr. Officially the A70, it's better known as the 'Lang Whang' ('long leather bootlace' in old Scots). Burke and Hare, the 19th-century grave robbers turned serial killers, carted their corpses along the Lang Whang on their way to sell them for research at the Edinburgh Medical College. Robert Burns was another frequent traveller, often stopping in Carnwath's Wee Bush Inn... where he scratched a window pane with the words, "Lang Whang, Lang Whang, Lang Bloody Whang!"

The A70 takes us to the east of Lanark, over the River Clyde and onto the open road to Rigside. Soon we're turning north, shadowing the motorway on the

old A74, now designated as a B-road, and steadily (and sadly) losing its last remaining stretches of dual carriageway. You'll probably have the road to yourself, so you can open the throttle as far as the speed limit allows to Lesmahagow. The section from Strathaven to Muirkirk is fun all the way, starting off with a long straight, then a bendy bit, before it opens out for a canter across the high ground. There's a little more work to do as you draw near to Muirkirk, but then the road invites you to select top gear as you point the front wheel back east. Soon after Douglas, you can cross under the motorway to head directly back to Biggar if you want to cut the expedition short, but we're turning south, back onto the old A74. It's hard not to feel blessed as you watch the trucks and cars jostle for position on the motorway, while you enjoy a clear, fast and empty road across the moors. The NC500 claims to be Scotland's

answer to Route 66, but really it's just a marketing slogan. In fact, the B7078/7076 is the nearest equivalent in Scotland – an abandoned highway that remains wide, fast, largely unused and hugely enjoyable.

At Abington there's a second chance to take a shortcut back to Biggar (by turning north after crossing the motorway and following signs), but in many ways the best is yet to come. We continue to shadow the motorway south, crossing into Dumfriesshire, until a sign to Greenhillstairs invites us to climb the hillside to cross into the River Annan valley, just north of Moffat. Now we're on one of Scotland's classic biking roads, the A701 that links Moffat to Edinburgh. This section is known as 'The Beef Tub' – after the hollow in the hills where the Johnstone family used to hide stolen cattle. The Johnstones were regarded as devils, and the hollow

– on the right as you reach the top of the valley – is known as 'The Devil's Beeftub'. The road surface might be a little indifferent from The Beef Tub to Broughton, but it's a glorious road nonetheless and a blast to ride. Then we turn left for a gentle cruise through the hills, a chance to unwind on the final few miles back to Biggar.

THE B7078, BY ELVAN WATER

WHAT TO SEE

New Lanark (ML11 9DB). An extraordinary, 19th-century mill complex, built in a gorge on the River Clyde and in operation until the 1960s. At its peak, 2,000 people lived and worked at New Lanark under the management of unusually enlightened owners. They enjoyed fair wages, affordable food, universal education and free healthcare. Just as remarkable is New Lanark's restoration, from near-dereliction in 1970 to being granted UNESCO World Heritage status in 2001. To visit requires a short detour. It is well signposted from the main roads around Lanark. Look out for signs from Direction No. 3.

LOOK OUT FOR

Football fans around Glenbuck (KA18 3SB). The old mining village has long since disappeared under a vast, opencast coal mine, but its football team – the Glenbuck Cherrypickers – once produced over 50 professional footballers, not least the great Liverpool manager, Bill Shankly. There's a memorial to Shankly et al at the roadside on the Glenbuck road, four miles east of Muirkirk.

WHERE TO STAY

The Elphinstone Hotel (ML12 6DL) is a traditional Scottish hotel on Biggar's main street and the town's oldest hostelry. Tidy, quirky, friendly and not unduly expensive.

Wee Row Hostel (ML11 9DJ) in New Lanark. Clean as a whistle, cheap as chips and slap bang in the middle of the World Heritage Site. Self-cater or nip across for a bar meal in the Mill Hotel.

WHERE TO EAT

The Mill Café (ML11 9DB) in New Lanark. If you're visiting the World Heritage Site, this is a handy place to grab a bite.

Route 74 Truckstop (ML11 0JN) at Lesmahagow. You can't beat a truckstop for a good plateful at trade prices. You won't leave any thinner, but you won't be hungry.

Stablestone Tea Room (ML11 0SF) in Glespin. There aren't many reasons to stop in Glespin, but this place is one of them. Nothing fancy, just good food at a sensible price.

1 In Biggar's High Street, head downhill, past the church spire

2 Turn right, onto the B7016 to Carnwath (8 miles)

3 Turn left onto the A70, and follow signs for Ayr, to traffic lights at Hyndford Bridge (7 miles)

4 Turn right, still on the A70, through Rigside, to roundabout before motorway (7 miles)

5 Turn right, onto the B7078, following signs to Lesmahagow (6 miles)

6 At roundabout opposite Tescos, turn left to T-junction (350 yards)

7 Turn right to Strathaven (8 miles)

8 At traffic lights, turn left onto A71, signed Kilmarnock, past Sainsbury's supermarket to roundabout (500 yards)

9 At next roundabout, turn left and left again soon after, following signs to Muirkirk (13 miles)

10 At traffic lights, turn left onto A70, to Douglas (10 miles)

11 Continue on A70 until you can see the motorway ahead (2 miles)

12 Just before a roundabout, turn right onto B7078, signed Abington (8 miles)

13 Turn left at roundabout to cross the motorway (350 yards)

14 Take 3rd exit at roundabout, onto A702 to Abington, and continue through the village to head south beside the motorway to roundabout (4 miles)

15 Go straight over roundabout, on A702, signed Elvanfoot, and continue to next roundabout (2.5 miles)

16 Go straight over roundabout, now on B7076, and continue south to road junction (7 miles)

17 Turn left onto B719 to Greenhillstairs and continue to T-junction (3 miles)

18 Turn left onto A701, signed Edinburgh, to Broughton (21 miles)

19 Turn left, onto B7016 to Biggar (5 miles)

HADDINGTON TO HAWICK

TWISTY	STRAIGHTER
SINGLE TRACK	WIDER

DISTANCE
125 miles

ALLOW
3.5 hours

THE MARKET SQUARE, KELSO

It was on the morning of 25 September 1915 that Piper Daniel Laidlaw from Berwickshire gave his greatest performance, near Loos in northern France.

The 7th Battalion of the King's Own Scottish Borderers were falling apart until the cry went up from their commanding officer, "Pipe them together, Laidlaw. For God's sake, pipe them together!" So the 40-year-old veteran climbed out of the trench, primed his pipes and struck up with *Blue Bonnets O'er The Border*, marching to and fro along the parapet. The lads rallied and the attack went ahead. Laidlaw got a VC and a leg wound for his troubles, along with a Croix de Guerre and the nickname, 'The Piper of Loos'. (It was a terrible day for the allies – no ground was gained and of the 12,000 men who went over the top, 8,000 were killed or injured.) Laidlaw was a quiet man, but remarkably brave – in short, he was a typical Borderer. Just like Jimmy Guthrie from Hawick, pre-eminent motorcycle racer in the 1930s but who liked nothing better than chatting about motorbikes and mechanics with visitors to the family business on the High Street. Or Steve Hislop (less quiet perhaps?), whose exploits on the track are still much talked

about 15 years after his death. And double Formula 1 champion Jim Clark (born in Fife but raised a Borderer), who many regard as the most naturally gifted driver ever to have raced a motor car.

We visit museums dedicated to all three on today's outing, beginning in the historic town of Haddington, just off the A1. First we nip north to Myreton Motor Museum; homely, unstuffy, full of interest and well worth the admission fee. Then we head through Pencaitland, where there's a memorial to local boy Jock Taylor, World Motorcycle Sidecar Champion, who died while racing in Finland in 1982. We cross the A68 to the prettier A7, with more bends, fewer speed cameras and less traffic. It's a

lovely run through the soft border hills to Hawick. Stopping to pay homage at the town's museum to Messrs Guthrie and Hislop, we're then heading through Denholm, muster point for the annual Jimmy Guthrie Memorial Run each June, and the Hizzy Run each August.

It's a fine road all the way to the A68 but, for excitement, we're heading 'over the Dunion', to approach Jedburgh from on high. Soon we're settled in top as we follow the River Teviot to Kelso, through the cobbled square on our way to Duns. This is Jim Clark country where, in spite of his international success, he felt most at home on the family farm in Chirnside. Fifty years after his death – in an accident at Hockenheim that is

still unexplained – a new museum is being opened to celebrate Clarke's life and achievements. Then we strike out northwards, across the rough uplands of the Lammermuir Hills on our way back to Haddington.

SOUNDTRACK

The Lammermuir Waltz by Freeland Barbour. A dance tune from one of Scotland's most influential accordionists.

FURTHER READING

Hizzy: The Autobiography of Steve Hislop (Willow, 2004)

WHAT TO SEE

Myreton Motor Museum (EH32 0PZ) feels more like an old workshop than a museum. Lots of cars, bikes and motorobilia and not a crowd control barrier in sight.

'**The Concorde Experience**' – it's the headline-grabbing exhibit at Scotland's National Museum of Flight (EH39 5LF) on the old wartime aerodrome at East Fortune.

'Clarty Hole', now known as **Abbotsford House**, near Melrose (TD6 9BQ). Sir Walter Scott bought a muddy farm and built a mighty mansion which he filled with quirky acquisitions. It's not far off our route and well signposted.

Wilton Lodge, Hawick (TD9 7LG) where the town's museum has displays honouring its most famous motorcycling sons, and fine statues in the grounds.

LOOK OUT FOR

Bike racing at East Fortune race track. The Melville Motorcycle Club runs a circuit on part of the old airfield (EH39 5LF) and motorcycle racing is held here several times a year.

Hume Castle is a 19th century folly built on the site of a 12th century castle. There's an outstanding view from the top. On a clear day you can see the border at the Carter Bar, where the A68 crests the hill to cross between Scotland and England.

WHERE TO STAY

Redshill Farm B&B in Gifford (EH41 4JN). Everything you could ask for except an evening meal, but there are pubs in nearby Gifford.

The Elm House Hotel (TD9 9BD) in Hawick is perfectly placed for the centre of town, with private parking round the back. The rooms are cheaper if you ask for the annexe.

WHERE TO EAT

The Loft Café (EH41 3DR) is just off Haddington's main street, behind the Corn Exchange. Good food with a strong emphasis on locally sourced produce.

↑ **1** From the centre of Haddington (EH41 3ED) facing the Town House:

←T **2** Leave the Town House to your right to traffic lights (350 yards)

↻ **3** Turn left into Hardgate to roundabout (0.5 mile)

←T **4** Go under the A1 and left on roundabout, signed Camptoun, to T-junction (3 miles)

↦ **5** Turn left onto B1371, signed Aberlady, to Motor Museum sign (0.5 mile)

↓ **6** Turn right to Myreton Motor Museum (1 mile)

↦ **7** Return to B1371 (1 mile)

←↻ **8** Turn right onto B1371 to roundabout (1 mile)

←↻ **9** Turn left onto A6137 to Haddington, over roundabout to T-junction (3 miles)

↟ **10** Go ahead onto A6093, through Pencaitland to T-junction (10 miles)

←T **11** Turn left onto A68, signed Jedburgh, to Pathhead (1 mile)

↦ **12** On entering the village, turn right onto B6367, signed Crichton, to T-junction (1.5 miles)

←T **13** Turn left for 100 yards, then turn right, signed Galashiels (3 miles)

←T **14** Turn left onto A7 and follow signs to Hawick (35 miles)

To visit Hawick Museum (TD9 7JL):
A At North Bridge roundabout (by Leisure Centre) turn right into Commercial Road, signed Carlisle (0.5 mile)
B As road bends left in front of a car park, turn right and then left to the museum (0.5 mile)
C Return to North Bridge roundabout to rejoin route (1 mile)

↻ **15** At roundabout, cross the river into Mart Street to next roundabout (350 yards)

←↻ **16** Take second left, signed Kelso, to Denholm (5 miles)

↑ **17** Continue on A698 to junction (2 miles)

↦ **18** Turn right onto B6358 to Jedburgh (4 miles)

←T **19** At T-junction at bottom of the High Street, turn left onto A68, signed Edinburgh (2 miles)

↱ **20** Turn right and right again onto A698, signed Kelso, to roundabout (9 miles)

←↻ **21** Turn left into town, leaving square to your right into Roxburgh Street (1 mile)

←T **22** At T-junction by castle gates, turn left, cross roundabout to junction (1 mile)

↱ **23** Turn left into B6364, signed Greenlaw, to T-junction (7 miles)

⊤↱ **24** Turn right into Greenlaw and follow signs to Duns (8 miles) (The Jim Clark Museum is on your left on the way into town)

↑ **25** With the Jim Clark Museum on your left, continue for 200 yards

←⊣ **26** Turn left onto Castle Street (1 mile)

↰ **27** Bear left to join B6355 to Gifford (20 miles)

↦ **28** After the church, turn right onto B6369 to T-junction in Haddington (4 miles)

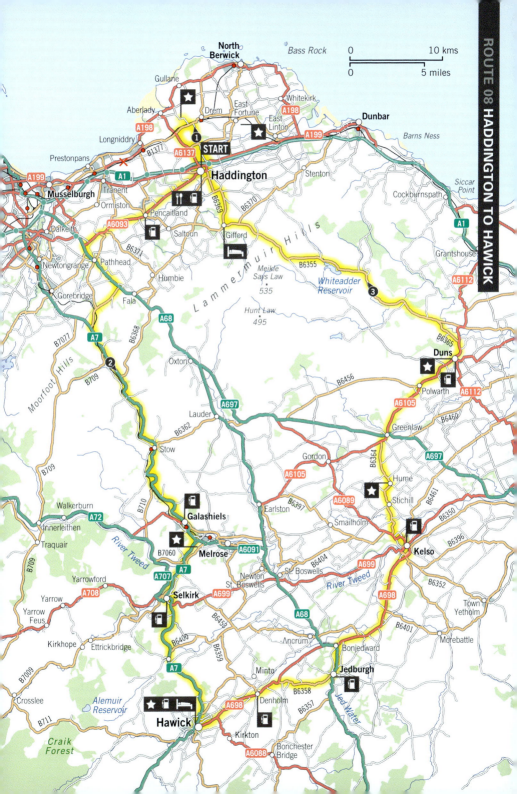

ARRAN

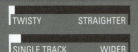

TWISTY — STRAIGHTER	**DISTANCE** 84 miles
SINGLE TRACK — WIDER	**ALLOW** 1 day

It's a guide book cliché to describe Arran as 'Scotland in miniature', and this book avoids clichés like the plague.

But it's true to say that the fault line that separates Scotland's highlands from the lowlands continues through Arran and has the same effect. Rugged, jagged mountains in the north, softer moorland in the south, all wrapped up in the wild remoteness we expect of a Scottish island. And as it's under an hour by ferry from Ayrshire's bustling west coast, it's remarkable that Arran is not busier than it is.

The road that hugs the shore makes a straightforward circuit (turn left off the ferry and continue for 55 miles until you're back where you started), but there are two passes over the hills at the southern end that have to be fitted into any meaningful exploration of the island. Even in this part of Scotland you can't escape Thomas Telford's work – in 1817 he devised the route for The String, a lovely pass that cuts across from Brodick to Blackwaterfoot. It saved travellers a lengthy journey round the southern shore in the 19th century and makes for a superb run for motorbikes in the 21st. Further south is another cross-island route, this time on a narrow, single track running from the south-west corner over to Lamlash.

CORRIE

Brodick, where the ferry connects with Ardrossan, is the official capital, but Lamlash is the main – and arguably the prettiest – settlement. Towards the south end, turn off the main road to loop through Kildonan, where the views to the Ayrshire coast and the islands of Pladda and Ailsa Craig are superb. Then we're heading up the less developed but no less beautiful east coast, always accompanied by superb views over Kilbrannan Sound to Kintyre, until we reach Lochranza. This is where the Vikings regrouped after their trouncing at the Battle of Largs in 1263 and where – or at least, where it is said – Hergé found his inspiration for Tintin's 'The Dark Island' adventure. Lochranza is a pretty little place, tucked in under the mountains with a castle sitting on a

shingle spit sticking out into the loch. It also has a summer ferry connecting to Cloanaig on Kintyre if you want to make Arran a stepping stone. Islay, Oban and Inveraray are all easily accessed from Claonaig on the other side.

Now the road takes a shortcut across the north-east corner, leaving the coast until we arrive at Sannox, for the last few miles down to Corrie and Brodick. Don't miss the views to Goat Fell on the way. It's only an hour by ferry from Ardrossan and you can buy a good breakfast on the boat! If you're planning to island hop, ask CalMac about their Hopscotch tickets, which combine fares for different routes. Arran is a fabulous place to visit and the roads are fun to ride, although not always

in great condition. As an introduction to Scotland's islands it's ideal and, for most of the population, it's remarkably convenient!

SOUNDTRACK

I Missed The Boat by Claire Hastings. If you've done it, you'll know the feeling.

FURTHER READING

The Legacy of Elizabeth Pringle by Kirsty Wark (Two Roads, 2014). In her will, Elizabeth Pringle leaves her house to a stranger, a young mother she'd seen pushing a pram down the road over 30 years previously. Now the baby in that pram is wondering why.

ROSS ROAD, ARRAN

WHAT TO SEE

Machrie Moor (KA27 8DT) is home to an impressive array of standing stones and stone circles dating back to Neolithic times.

Not far away is **King's Cave** (KA27 8DX), one of several in Scotland where it's said Robert the Bruce saw the spider that encouraged him to try, try and try again. This is probably the most impressive of the contenders. Park on the left and follow the path down to the shore. If you come back the same way, it takes about an hour.

LOOK OUT FOR

Potholes. And **seals** on the shore at Kildonan (KA27 8SD).

WHERE TO STAY

The Lagg Hotel (KA27 8PQ) near Kilmory can claim to be the oldest hotel in Arran. It's charmingly traditional, with log fires, extensive gardens and a lovely setting.

Castlekirk Arthouse B&B (KA27 8HL) in Lochranza's old Free Kirk. Breakfast with a view!

WHERE TO EAT

Fiddlers Bar and Grill (KA27 8AJ) in Brodick offers good food and a chance to hear some live music.

The Sandwich Station (KA27 8HL) near the pier in Lochranza. Terrific sandwiches, and the soup is not bad either!

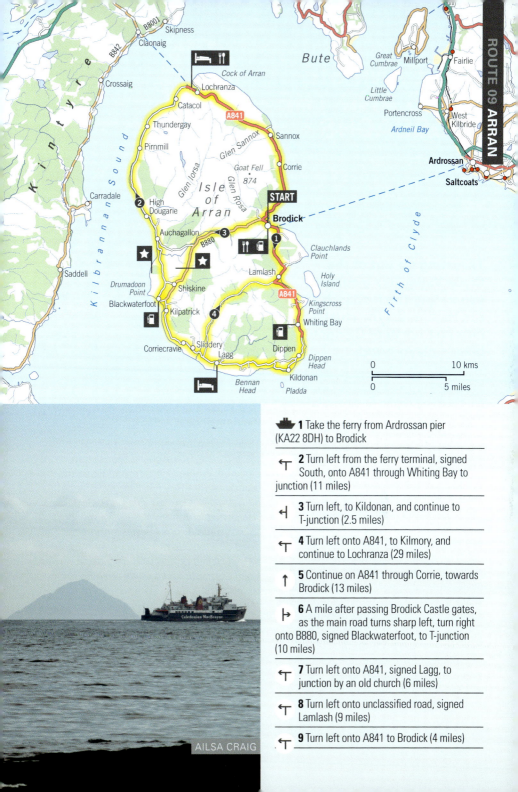

B8001
Skipness
Claonaig
B842
Crossaig
Kintyre

Cock of Arran
Lochranza
Catacol
A841
Thundergay
Pirnmill

Bute
Great Cumbrae
Millport
Fairlie
Little Cumbrae
Portencross
West Kilbride
Ardneil Bay

Ardrossan
Saltcoats

Sannox
Corrie
Glen Sannox
Goat Fell
874

Glen Iorsa
Glen Rosa
Isle of Arran

Carradale
High Dougarie
Auchagallon
B880
START
Brodick

Clauchlands Point
Holy Island
Firth of Clyde

Saddell
Kilbrannan Sound

Shiskine
Lamlash
A841
Kingscross Point

Drumadoon Point
Blackwaterfoot
Kilpatrick
Whiting Bay

Corriecravie
Sliddery
Lagg
Dippen

Dippen Head
Kildonan
Pladda
Bennan Head

0   10 kms
0   5 miles

AILSA CRAIG

🚢 **1** Take the ferry from Ardrossan pier (KA22 8DH) to Brodick

↰ **2** Turn left from the ferry terminal, signed South, onto A841 through Whiting Bay to junction (11 miles)

↲ **3** Turn left, to Kildonan, and continue to T-junction (2.5 miles)

↰ **4** Turn left onto A841, to Kilmory, and continue to Lochranza (29 miles)

↑ **5** Continue on A841 through Corrie, towards Brodick (13 miles)

↳ **6** A mile after passing Brodick Castle gates, as the main road turns sharp left, turn right onto B880, signed Blackwaterfoot, to T-junction (10 miles)

↰ **7** Turn left onto A841, signed Lagg, to junction by an old church (6 miles)

↰ **8** Turn left onto unclassified road, signed Lamlash (9 miles)

↰ **9** Turn left onto A841 to Brodick (4 miles)

THE CAMPSIE FELLS AND THE TROSSACHS

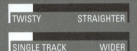

TWISTY   STRAIGHTER

SINGLE TRACK   WIDER

DISTANCE
107 miles

ALLOW
3.5 hours

THE DUKE'S PASS

Thrusting up out of the Clyde Valley like a curtain separating the lowlands from the Highlands, the cluster of hills just north of Glasgow is a biker's playground.

The Campsie Fells and Fintry Hills may lack a little height, but there's plenty of fun to be had on the roads that weave over and around them. And they act as our gateway to the Trossachs – more famous, more busy and more like mountains.

We're starting from Kilsyth, easily accessible from the M90 (J7), and just a few miles north of Glasgow if you're coming through the city. It seems slightly perverse to start off uphill on a road called Tak-Ma-Doon, but it's a lovely – if narrow – climb out of Kilsyth… although you may have to share it with cyclists testing themselves against the gradient. On a clear day, you can see the Forth bridges and the Wallace Monument from the summit viewpoint before you let the road tak-ya-doon into the Carron Valley, crossing a shallow ford on the way. It's wider and faster past the Carron Reservoir – unusually, it has a dam at both ends – as we head through Fintry following the

river valley, the road narrowing gradually the further west we go.

Then it's northward on the main A81 towards the Trossachs, a tourist trap since Sir Walter Scott immortalised the legend of Rob Roy MacGregor. Branded an outlaw but lauded as a hero, Rob Roy has certainly done wonders for the local tourist trade. From Aberfoyle there's a dead-end (but dead-scenic) detour up to Inversnaid on the eastern side of Loch Lomond, and a quick nip across to the west side of Loch Katrine before returning to Aberfoyle. Now we're opening the throttle to climb hairpin bends onto the Duke's Pass, a glorious road through the hills, built by the Duke of Montrose in the 19th century to improve access to his estate. It was later upgraded for the convenience of Victorian tourists drawn to the area by Scott's epic poem, 'The Lady of the

Lake', set around Loch Katrine. The road is beautiful but it's also popular so, if you're following a caravan for a few miles, blame Sir Walter. There's another detour – shorter, but also a dead end – to Loch Katrine and the chance to see the steamship that runs excursions on the loch, before we turn east. The road twists its way along the water's edge with relatively few overtaking opportunities, through Brig o'Turk, until we draw nearer Callander. The A84 will take you straight to Stirling if you prefer, but this route turns south in the middle of the town. We follow the main road for only a couple of miles before moving onto the B822, which leads us out across Flanders Moss National Nature Reserve. It's fast and flat to Thornhill and beyond over the farmland that straddles the River Forth – high gears and relatively traffic-free all the way. Then, the big finale – the Crow Road!

It's a superb run, climbing slowly and steadily to the summit, then a moorland pass to the top of the Campsie Glen. From here it's an enthralling descent, the road cut into the escarpment as it leads us back off the fells and into Lennoxtown, just a few miles west of the start.

SOUNDTRACK

Hang The Noose by Woodenbox With A Fistful of Fivers. Scottish? Country? Spaghetti western? All these and more.

FURTHER READING

The Crow Road by Iain Banks (Abacus, 1992). It's a different Crow Road to the one that brings us into Lennoxtown, but don't let that put you off.

IN THE TROSSACHS

WHAT TO SEE

The steamship Sir Walter Scott runs excursions on Loch Katrine (FK17 8HZ). It's a lovely loch, although you board at a rather commercialised (i.e. not very attractive) part of it. The steamship is magnificent; it was built on the Clyde in 1899, then dismantled and reassembled on Loch Katrine the following year. Sadly, her owners added a monstrous 'passenger lounge' onto the forward deck in 2007.

LOOK OUT FOR

The entrance into the **Three Lochs Forest Drive** (FK8 3SY) is just a couple of miles north of Aberfoyle. It's a six-mile detour on an unsurfaced forestry track, which provides a refreshing change, particularly if the main road is busy. You emerge back on our route before a turn-off to Loch Katrine. It's only open in the summer and there's a small fee involved.

WHERE TO STAY

Allanfauld Farm (G65 9DF) in Kilsyth is an oasis of calm and hospitality. Very near the start and the sort of breakfast you'd expect from a farmhouse!

Auchenlaich (FK17 8LQ), Callander, is another farmhouse B&B. They'll do an evening meal too if you ask them. And you can get your bike under cover.

WHERE TO EAT

Brig o'Turk Tearoom & Restaurant (FK17 8HT) opened to cater for cyclists in 1923, and it's been in the same wooden shack ever since. Something of an institution, and it's easy to see why.

The Pier Café (FK8 3TY) in Stronachlachar is perched on the edge of Loch Katrine. It's at the dead-end of a long run up from Aberfoyle. A quick snack or a proper meal in a lovely setting.

1 From the Coachman Hotel (G65 0SP) in Kilsyth, put the hotel on your left

2 Head along Stirling Road for 400 yards

3 Turn left, signed Carronbridge, onto Tak-Ma-Doon Road (4 miles)

4 Turn left onto B818 and follow signs to Fintry (9 miles)

5 Continue ahead on B818 to Killearn (7 miles)

6 Just before the church turn right onto Station Road (1 mile)

7 Turn right on roundabout onto A81 and follow signs to Aberfoyle (11 miles)

8 Continue ahead in Aberfoyle onto B829 to T-junction (11 miles)

9 Turn left for Inversnaid (4 miles) and right for Stronachlachar (800 yards)

10 Return to Aberfoyle (11 miles)

11 Turn left onto A821, signed Callander, to T-junction (13 miles)

12 Turn right onto A84 to Callander (1 mile)

13 Turn right onto A81, signed Glasgow (2 miles)

14 Where main road bends right, continue ahead onto B822 to Thornhill, Kippen, Fintry and Lennoxtown (23 miles)

15 Turn right for Strathblane (5 miles) or left to return to Kilsyth (6 miles)

ROUTE 11
TYNDRUM, CRINAN AND SEIL

TWISTY ▮▮▮▯ STRAIGHTER	**DISTANCE** 150 miles
SINGLE TRACK ▮▮▯▯ WIDER	**ALLOW** 4.5 hours

Today's new word is 'petrosomatoglyph'. We're off to see one (or at least to ride past a place where there is one).

A petrosomatoglyph is a representation of a body part in stone and this is possibly the most important petrosomatoglyphic site in the country. South of Loch Awe, a rocky outcrop at Dunadd was once the capital of the ancient kingdom of Dalriada – a carved footprint on a stone slab on the summit is where the kings were 'crowned', except they didn't have crowns in those days. By putting his foot in it, the new king was cementing his commitment to the land and pledging to do his best for his people. Climb the knoll and you can place your motorbike boot in the very spot where Kenneth MacAlpin – who united the Scots and the Picts to become the first king of a united Scotland – (probably) put his foot. They must have had smaller feet in those days. Or wee kings.

To get there, we set off west along the A85 – which is made for sports bikes – travelling through the Pass of Brander where the road is built out over the loch like some continental super-highway. Then we turn down the west

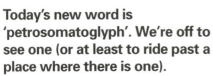
BELLANOCH, NEAR CRINAN

side of Loch Awe, Scotland's longest freshwater loch. It's a tighter road, but more fun and better visibility than the A road on the eastern bank – plenty of ups and downs, twists and turns, through woodlands and scattered communities to Kilmartin. From here you can wind things up a little on the well-surfaced highway through Kilmartin Glen. If we were on a walking holiday, we'd probably linger here for a bit, among the chambered cairns, cists, standing stones and rock carvings. But we're here to ride, so it's on to Dunadd, where you really should stop to look at the hill fort. The signage is pitiful for such an important site but you'll see it on the right soon after you pass the turn-off for Crinan Ferry (a lovely spot but without a ferry). Next, we follow the Crinan Canal for a bit – don't be surprised if you come round a corner to see a yacht approaching! Crinan, where the canal

enters the Sound of Jura, is a joy for anyone interested in boats. It's a lovely place to wander along the towpath or sit by the lock gates to soak up the atmosphere.

The route home begins in an unusually straight line for Argyll, as we cross Mòine Mhòr, a raised bog that the Gaels called 'The Great Moss'. Then we go back through Kilmartin Glen, passing Loch Craignish and Loch Melfort to Seil, and 'The Bridge over the Atlantic'. Seil is an island thanks to the Clachan Sound, a narrow strip of tidal water that opens into the Atlantic at both ends and crossed by a 19th century hump-backed bridge. It's a lovely scenic run to Ellenabeich, as close as we can get to Easdale Island without getting onto a boat. Easdale is the venue for the annual World Skimming Championships, which put the old slate quarries to good use. Then it's back over the bridge,

along the banks of Loch Feochan to Oban. With its lookalike-Colosseum on the hill, and busy harbour, Oban is one of the hotspots of Scottish tourism and a main ferry port for the islands to the west. It also marks the beginning of the end of this outing, as we head out past Dunstaffnage and through Connel before selecting top gear for the run back to Tyndrum.

SOUNDTRACK

Island Boy – Trail West. A hare-um, scare-um, devil may care-um ceilidh band from Tiree. Upbeat traditional music to fill the dance floor.

FURTHER READING

The Deadman's Pedal by Alan Warner (Jonathan Cape, 2012). A 'coming of age' novel set in a town not unlike Oban.

CRINAN

WHAT TO SEE

Take a trip into the **'hollow mountain'** at Ben Cruachan (PA33 1AN) where a vast, man-made cavern forms part of an ingenious and pioneering electricity scheme. Water pours down the hillside during the day through turbines that generate power. Then at night, when demand is lower, the turbines are reversed and pump water back up the hill. It's like a set from James Bond. Tours can be booked in advance.

For some older technology, stop in at the well-preserved **Bonawe Ironworks** (PA35 1JQ), an extraordinary piece of 18th century industrial heritage to find in the Scottish Highlands. For over 100 years iron ore was brought from Cumbria to Bonawe for smelting due to the plentiful supply of charcoal in the area. Just beyond it is the peaceful **Taynuilt Pier**.

LOOK OUT FOR

VIC 32 if she's at home in the basin at Crinan (PA31 8SR). She's one of the few surviving Clyde 'puffers' that were once common on Scotland's west coast, and one of only two in Scotland still powered by steam. The other, VIC 27, is round the corner in the Crinan boatyard undergoing a lengthy restoration. VIC 32 now operates as a diminutive cruise liner on Scotland's west coast. On a few days a year, she offers one-hour 'trips around the bay'. You might be lucky!

WHERE TO STAY

Innish B&B (PA34 4QZ) faces you as you cross Clachan Bridge – over the Atlantic – onto Seil Island. Lovely setting, nice rooms, full Scottish breakfast and only a few yards away from the 18th century Tigh-an-Truish Inn, where Jacobite islanders used to change out of their kilts before crossing the sound to the mainland. Tigh-a-Truish means 'House of Trousers'.

Corran House (PA34 5PN) in Oban offers a mixture of double, twin and bunk-room accommodation. Breakfast is extra. There's a lovely view from the front windows and it's very handy for Markie Dan's pub – it's in the basement.

WHERE TO EAT

The Green Welly (FK20 8RY) is popular with tourists but almost a compulsory stop for bikers! There's food, fuel and a gift shop. And there's always something of interest going on or passing by.

The **Oyster Bar & Restaurant** (PA34 4RQ) in Ellenabeich, Seil. A seafood place, naturally, but also offering burgers, chicken, etc. Friendly, family run and in a fabulous setting. Nothing fancy about the prices either!

Or try the **Seafood Shack** (PA34 4DB) by the ferry terminal in Oban. It's legendary and for good reason.

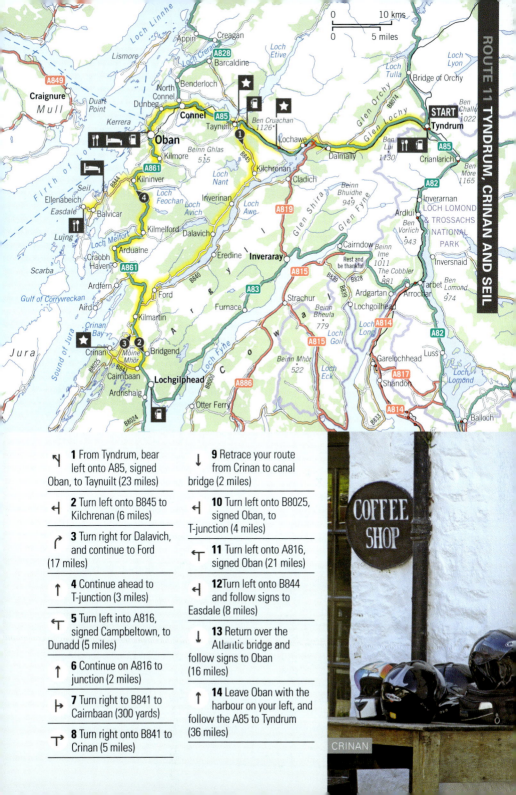

1 From Tyndrum, bear left onto A85, signed Oban, to Taynuilt (23 miles)

2 Turn left onto B845 to Kilchrenan (6 miles)

3 Turn right for Dalavich, and continue to Ford (17 miles)

4 Continue ahead to T-junction (3 miles)

5 Turn left into A816, signed Campbeltown, to Dunadd (5 miles)

6 Continue on A816 to junction (2 miles)

7 Turn right to B841 to Cairnbaan (300 yards)

8 Turn right onto B841 to Crinan (5 miles)

9 Retrace your route from Crinan to canal bridge (2 miles)

10 Turn left onto B8025, signed Oban, to T-junction (4 miles)

11 Turn left onto A816, signed Oban (21 miles)

12 Turn left onto B844 and follow signs to Easdale (8 miles)

13 Return over the Atlantic bridge and follow signs to Oban (16 miles)

14 Leave Oban with the harbour on your left, and follow the A85 to Tyndrum (36 miles)

CRINAN

LOCH LOMOND TO GLENCOE

▮ TWISTY — STRAIGHTER	⦿ **DISTANCE** 190 miles	
▮ SINGLE TRACK — WIDER	🕑 **ALLOW** 4 hours	

GLENCOE

There's no two ways about it, the A82 between Tyndrum and Glencoe is fabulous!

It seems to have been tailor-made for the motorcycle and, unlike other sections of the A82, traffic doesn't spoil the fun. It's a classic road with awe-inspiring scenery, a good grippy surface, speedy straights and beguiling corners. What's more, on this outing it's just one of several majestic roads... each different but each utterly enthralling.

We're starting from Balloch, at the southern end of Loch Lomond and, although you might choose to head up the bonnie bonnie banks to Tarbet, the road is busy, the overtaking opportunities are few and its safety record is poor. Instead, we're turning off after a few miles onto the Haul Road, which was built to service the submarine base at Faslane – the route is wide, free-flowing and virtually empty. There's little chance to relax up the side of Loch Long because the road lifts and dips over blind summits, twisting like a big dipper through the trees. At Arrochar we can relax a little as we cut back across to Loch Lomond for a few winding miles in heavy traffic before the bends begin to ease and the road starts to loosen up. From Tyndrum, we climb steadily up through the narrow

glen before the long downhill to Bridge of Orchy. Soon we're climbing again up the Black Mount and onto Rannoch Moor, heather and lochans on either side and a truly glorious road ahead. Just after the ski centre, the entrance to Glen Etive appears on the left – much loved by motoring journalists and James Bond fans (part of the movie Skyfall was filmed here). The mountains close in as we enter Glencoe – superb in sunshine but perhaps most atmospheric when the hills are shrouded with mist. Glencoe was the scene of the notorious massacre in 1692 when troops under the command of a Campbell accepted several days of hospitality from the MacDonalds of Glencoe... before killing them in the night. Now we head round Loch Leven, a sleepy backwater since the bridge was built at Ballachulish,

but today it's a spectacular road to the southern shore and back by the northern. Over the Ballachulish Bridge and south, we follow the coast to Appin, with a view to Castle Stalker – of Monty Python and The Holy Grail fame. There's an opportunity for another loch-side detour around Loch Creran if you want to eke out the journey, as we make for the bridge at Connel. Oban is five miles to the right, but we're heading left, through Taynuilt and along the top of Loch Awe for a right turn leading over the hill and down to Inveraray. After shooting the breeze with the bikers at the pier, the run back to Arrochar is equally thrilling, hugging the shoreline then running between steep hills and over the Rest and Be Thankful. From Arrochar, you can either cross to Tarbet and head down Loch

Lomond-side – a good option if it's late in the day (when the traffic is light) – or retrace the outbound route back to Balloch on the Haul Road. Heads you win, tails you don't lose!

SOUNDTRACK

The Massacre of Glencoe, sung by Alastair McDonald. Several people have recorded it, but he's got the best surname for the job.

FURTHER READING

Glencoe: The Story of the Massacre by John Prebble (Penguin, 1973). What happened to cause it and what happened because of it, expertly explained and very readable.

↑ **1** From the Stoneymollan (Balloch) roundabout on the A82 (G83 8QS) – the one with the geese sculpture in the middle – head north, signed Crianlarich (5 miles)

← **2** Turn left onto A817, signed Gairlochhead (9 miles)

↱ **3** Turn right on roundabout onto A814, signed Arrochar (1.5 miles)

↱ **4** Go right on roundabout (unsigned) to Arrochar (9 miles)

↦ **5** Turn right onto A83, signed Crianlarich, to Tarbet (1.5 miles)

← **6** Turn left onto A82, signed Crianlarich, and follow A82 to Glencoe (52 miles)

↦ **7** Turn right onto B863 to Kinlochleven (7 miles)

↑ **8** Continue on B863 to junction at North Ballachulish (9 miles)

← **9** Turn left for Oban to roundabout (1 mile)

↰ **10** Turn left onto A828 to junction after crossing Connel Bridge (26 miles)

↦ **11** Turn right onto A85, signed Crianlarich, to junction 1.5 miles after the Loch Awe Hotel (18 miles)

↦ **12** Turn right onto A819 to Inveraray (14 miles)

↰ **13** Turn left onto A83, signed Glasgow, to Arrochar (22 miles)
Note: To avoid Loch Lomond, bear right in Arrochar onto A814, then go first left on two roundabouts and turn right onto A82 to Balloch (24 miles)

↑ **14** Continue on A83 to Tarbet, then turn right onto A82 to Balloch (16 miles)

WHAT TO SEE

Kilchurn Castle (PA33 1AF), at the head of Loch Awe, was once an island fortress, but was abandoned in the 18th century after being struck by lightning. Climb to the top to enjoy the views, but don't leave without appreciating what looks like a tiered podium in the courtyard. It's actually the base of a turret that was blown off the tower by the lightning strike in 1760 and landed upside down, still in one piece. Access to the castle is from a car park off the A85. It's on the left soon after joining the A85.

LOOK OUT FOR

People driving (or riding) badly. The road causes frustration and some folk do daft things. And tourists are inclined to stop without warning to take a photograph, or dive up a side road.

WHERE TO STAY

The Drovers Inn (G83 7DX), Inverarnan. More than 300 years old, and still going strong, so they must be doing something right. Full of character and humour, it's the only place in Scotland with a stuffed grizzly bear in reception. Probably.

WHERE TO EAT

The Three Villages Café (G83 7AB) in Arrochar is a popular biker's stop. It used to be the Pit Stop Diner. Lovely setting and good grub!

The Green Welly Stop (FK20 8RY), Tyndrum. Café/gift shop/petrol station with a dedicated parking area for motorbikes. There's even a bucket and sponge to wipe the midges off your visor.

Clachaig Inn (PH49 4HX) in Glencoe is an atmospheric old hostelry that will probably be full of climbers and walkers. It's close to the site of the massacre, and there's a sign at the reception desk to say they won't serve Campbells. (Just Heinz or Batchelors, then?)

'Cakes in the Call Box' (PA33 1BQ) at Cladich. The only things you'll find in this old red telephone kiosk are freshly baked scones and fancies, and a Tupperware honesty box. If only they could manage a coffee machine as well, it would be perfect.

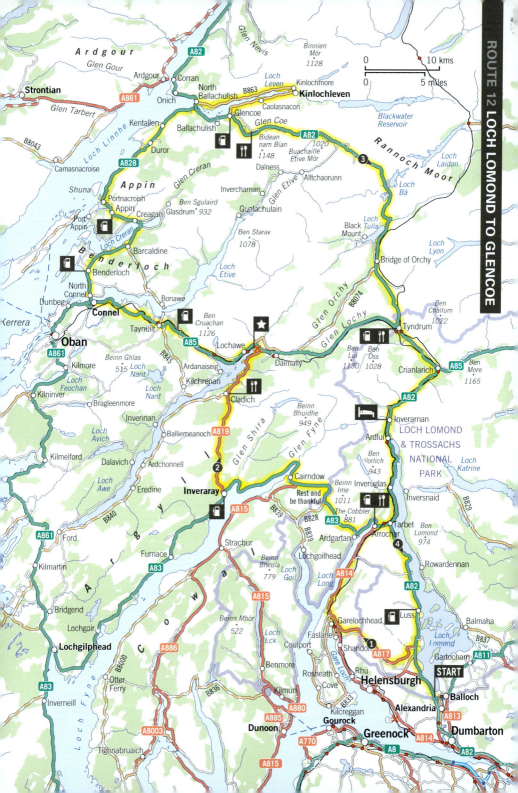

MULL

TWISTY	STRAIGHTER
SINGLE TRACK	WIDER

DISTANCE
123 miles

ALLOW
1 day

First things first: don't go to Mull expecting wide carriageways and fast corners.

Barring a stretch between Tobermory and Craignure, Mull's roads are entirely single track. This is a very much a scenic outing, not a sporting one! That said, the island is a great place to explore, with a wild and empty interior surrounded by a rocky, rugged shoreline, punctuated by isolated settlements hugging the shore. The ferry from Oban makes landfall at Craignure, just along the coast from the MacLean stronghold of Duart Castle. The MacLeans had a habit of backing the wrong side – first they plotted against James VI, then they teamed up with the Royalists against Cromwell and the final straw came when they joined the Jacobite Rebellion in 1689. It resulted in the estates being forfeited and Duart Castle was in ruins by the time the clan chief bought it back and restored it in 1911. Now, still owned by the MacLeans, much of the castle is open to the public.

After passing Loch Spelve, there's an opportunity to detour to Loch Buie, with standing stones and the derelict Moy Castle the headline attractions at the far end of the eight-mile, single track road. Then we're heading up through the trees to the barren and isolated Glen More. Single track it may be over the

LOCH NA KEAL, MULL

moorland, but it's a decent road with plenty of visibility ahead. Fionnphort is another dead-end detour, but few people pass up on the chance to take the ferry to visit Iona, 'the cradle of Christianity in Scotland'. Now we're heading north beside Loch Scridain before turning inland, climbing through forestry to cross the Ardmeanach peninsula. The open moor affords plenty of opportunities to stop and enjoy the magnificent views over Ulva to Coll and Tiree. The road is tucked under cliffs as we join Loch na Keal for a lovely run to Gruline, where Mull is pinched to a narrow waist. Bear right for the shortest route back to the ferry, or left onto the B8073 for Calgary, following the north

side of the loch and looking across the water to Ben More, Mull's highest peak. The views are magnificent, with only a short section of rather dull moorland in the middle, as we make our way to Calgary, well known for its white sands and Canadian namesake. After Dervaig, a series of hairpin bends lift us over the hillside for the run into Tobermory, Mull's multicoloured, picture-postcard capital. From the island's solitary roundabout, we head down the wider A848 for several refreshing miles beside the Sound of Mull. It narrows again before opening up for the finale from Salen to Craignure, including a novel stretch of single track dual-carriageway at Pennygown. If you're heading north from Mull, you might want to consider getting the ferry from Fishnish to Lochaline, which offers a short cut to Ardnamurchan and Mallaig.

SOUNDTRACK

This Little Sister by The Mull Historical Society (a.k.a Colin MacIntyre). N.B. To avoid any confusion, the local history group in Mull is called The Mull Historical and Archaeological Society.

FURTHER READING

Kidnapped by Robert Louis Stevenson. (Penguin, 2007). The tale of David Balfour's kidnapping and shipwreck on Mull. Based on real events and characters of the time.

TOBERMORY

WHAT TO SEE

From Fionnphort, take the ferry to Iona to visit the **abbey** (PA76 6SQ). It's been a place of pilgrimage since St Columba founded a monastery on Iona in 563. Repeatedly sacked by the Vikings, but always restored or rebuilt, it's the burial place of over 50 kings and queens, mostly Scottish but a handful of Scandinavian and Irish as well. Only essential vehicles are allowed on the ferry (your bike doesn't qualify!) but it's a lovely walk up to the abbey.

LOOK OUT FOR

Falsehoods. Calgary in Canada didn't get its name because disposed crofters from Calgary (Mull) settled there following the Highland Clearances. The truth is more mundane. When the Mounties wanted to rename a fort in 1875, Calgary was suggested by a soldier, Col. James Macleod, who had once visited Calgary House on Mull.

WHERE TO STAY

Arle Lodge (PA72 6JS) between Tobermory and Salen – not luxurious but basic, clean and nicely quirky. Somewhere between a hotel and a B&B. **The Craignure Inn** (PA65 6AY) is an old drover's inn close to the main ferry terminal. A pub with a few rooms, good menu and hearty breakfast.

WHERE TO EAT

Summon the ferry for the short trip over to eat at **The Boathouse** on Ulva (PA73 6LZ). They land the shellfish from the family fishing boat, do all the baking themselves and serve a great selection of soups, rolls and daily specials. Mondays to Friday from April, and Sundays throughout June, July and August. Closed in October to the end of March.

The **fish van** on Tobermory's Fishermen's Pier (PA75 6NX) is popular with locals and crews from visiting yachts.

If it's raining, head for **Macgochans** (PA75 6NR) where you'll get good food and the chance of some live music too.

ROUTE 13 MULL

From the ferry

1 Turn left on the A849 to Fionnphort (Iona Ferry) (37 miles)

2 Return to road junction, signed Gruline (18 miles)

3 Turn left onto B8035 to Gruline (18 miles)

4 Fork left onto B8073, through Dervaig to Tobermory (31 miles)

5 From Tobermory's Main Street, put the sea to your left

6 Follow the A848, through Salen to Craignure (21 miles)

DUART CASTLE

RANNOCH AND GLEN LYON

TWISTY ▮▮▮▮ STRAIGHTER	📍 **DISTANCE** 180 miles	
SINGLE TRACK ▮ WIDER	⏱ **ALLOW** 1 day	

Rannoch is not quite the most remote railway station in the country, but it's probably the easiest remote station to get to without a train ticket.

And the road south out of Glen Lyon, might not be the loneliest road in the country, but you'd struggle to find a lonelier road with bigger potholes. Or another public road with gates! This outing takes us to the geographic centre of Scotland: if you draw a target on a map of Scotland, we're hitting the bullseye. Our starting point is Crieff, easily reached from Perth, Lochearnhead or, if you are coming from the south, through Greenloaning and Braco on the Perthshire Tourist Route which seeks to lure people off the dual carriageway. General Wade's old military road leads up through Crieff and the Sma' Glen before we turn left by Amulree. Glen Quaich is like a softened Bealach Na' Ba – more 'Pass of the Sheep' than 'Pass of the Cattle' – as we climb up onto the moor. Then a series of hairpin bends bring us down to Kenmore. Loch Tay is to the west, but we're heading east, along the River Tay to Aberfeldy and Grandtully. Then we cross an old railway bridge into Logierait to a single track road (without passing places) into Pitlochry. It's over 100 miles

THE SCHIEHALLION ROAD

until we next pass a petrol pump, so take the chance to top up the tank on the way into town.

After a few miles on the old A9 towards Killiecrankie, we're following the tortuously glorious B8019 up the Tummel Valley, always wary about meeting a tour bus on a corner. Before long, we're no longer looking down on Loch Tummel but almost touching the water's edge on Loch Rannoch. There's a fine view across the loch to Schiehallion, one of Scotland's most distinctive mountains. Schiehallion should be Gaelic for "shaped like a cone", but in fact it means something like "Fairy Hill of the Caledonians". Then we've a few pleasurable miles across Rannoch Moor to the station,

surrounded by wilderness but with a tea room on the platform to provide welcome refreshment.

Our homeward leg begins along the south side of Loch Rannoch to turn right, across the shoulder of Schiehallion and along the north bank of Loch Tay. Before long we're climbing the lower slopes of Ben Lawers, powering up to the reservoir at Lawers Dam and over into Glen Lyon – promoted as 'Scotland's longest, loneliest and loveliest' glen. When the even larger dam holding back Loch Lyon prevents us going further, we head south. Now the road is rough, with conjoined potholes, gravel dunes and a couple of gates. Yes, it is a public road and yes, it'll give your motorbike a good ol'

shaking! Once you're down in the valley it's a better road to Killin, and a great open highway back along Loch Earn to Comrie and home to Crieff. This route is easily broken down into sections if you want a shorter day.

↑ **1** From James Square in the centre of Crieff, put the memorial fountain to your right and head uphill, following the A85 to Gilmerton (2 miles)

← **2** Turn left onto A822, signed Dunkeld (10 miles)

← **3** Just before Amulree, turn left to Glen Quaich (11 miles)

↦ **4** At junction (below hairpin bends) turn right and then right again onto A827 to Aberfeldy (6 miles)

↑ **5** Continue on A827, through Grandtully, ignoring the bridge leading left and follow the unclassified road to Balnaguard (8 miles)

← **6** After Balnaguard, take the first turning on the left by stone cottage (1.5 miles)

↑ **7** Cross old railway bridge to T-junction (0.5 mile)

← **8** Turn left (150 yards)

↦ **9** Just past Logierait Inn, turn right (NB: The corner is steep!) (150 yards)

↑ **10** Follow the narrow road – without passing places – to T-junction (4 miles) (To avoid this narrow road, turn right after crossing the old railway bridge and follow signs to Pitlochry)

↱ **11** Turn right and follow signs into Pitlochry (1 mile)

↑ **12** Continue on A924 through Pitlochry, signed Tummel Bridge (2.5 miles)

← **13** Turn left on B8109 and follow signs to Kinloch Rannoch (16 miles)

↑ **14** Continue ahead to Rannoch Station (16 miles)

↓ **15** From Rannoch Station, head back the way you came to reach the first turning on your right, signed South Loch Rannoch (5 miles)

↦ **16** Turn right and follow the road beside the loch (11 miles)

↱ **17** At the end of the loch, bear right to T-junction (1 mile)

↱ **18** Turn right to T-junction (8 miles)

↱ **19** Turn right, signed Aberfeldy (4 miles)

↦ **20** Turn right to Fortingall and continue to T-junction (5 miles). **Note:** After Fortingall a sign points right to Glen Lyon. It's a lovely route and shorter, but misses out the invigorating climb to the Lawers dam. Both routes meet at Bridge of Balgie (No.23 below) where you should continue ahead to Loch Lyon.

↱ **21** Turn right, signed Killin (8 miles)

↦ **22** Turn right to Bridge of Balgie. If you miss the first turning, there's a second chance 300 yards later (9 miles) **Note:** The section after Pubil is not ideal (!) for sports bikes. If you prefer to avoid rough roads, miss out the loop through Glen Lyon and continue ahead on the A827 to Killin. Rejoin the Route Directions at No.26.

← **23** At T-junction, turn left to Loch Lyon (9 miles)

↑ **24** Continue and head over the bridge onto a rough, potholed road. After passing through gates, the road turns left in a valley to reach a T-junction (12 miles)

↱ **25** Turn right onto A827, through Killin to T-junction (3 miles)

← **26** Turn left onto A85 and follow signs back to Crieff (24 miles)

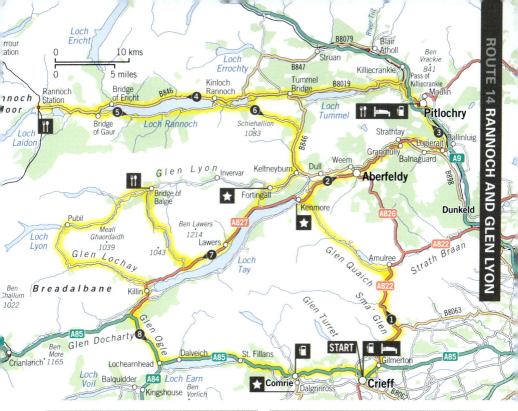

WHAT TO SEE

The Scottish Crannog Centre (PH15 2HY) in Kenmore shows what Iron Age life was like for people who lived on man-made islands. The centre has a reconstructed prehistoric roundhouse, sitting on stilts out in the loch (closed in winter).

The Fortingall Yew (PH15 2LL) is claimed to be the oldest living thing in Europe. There's less of it than there used to be, but it's remarkable it's here at all.

Cultybraggan Camp (PH6 2AB) near Comrie accommodated 4,000 SS, Marine Corps and Wermacht POWs during the Second World War. It's the last surviving example of a high-security prisoner of war camp in the UK.

LOOK OUT FOR

Timber trucks and tour buses on the B8019. They can give this lovely road an extra element of surprise.

WHERE TO STAY

Galvelbeg House (PH7 3EQ) in Crieff is biker-friendly and has great food, with an emphasis on home-made fare.

Westlands (PH16 5AR) in Pitlochry is a very welcoming, family-run B&B. Clean rooms, great breakfast and just a short walk from the town centre.

WHERE TO EAT

Pitlochry is full of eating places. The **Escape Route Café** (PH16 5BX) as you enter the town from the south is pretty good. The staff are friendly, the food is freshly prepared and the final bill doesn't make your eyes water.

Rannoch Station Tea Room (PA17 2QA). You'll have earned some refreshment after the miles you cover to get here. Is there a more isolated or delightful tea room in the country?

Glen Lyon Post Office and Tearoom (PH16 2PP). Splendidly set on the roadside and the only cuppa for miles around.

ROUTE 15

THE ANGUS GLENS

TWISTY	STRAIGHTER
SINGLE TRACK	WIDER

DISTANCE
185 miles

ALLOW
1 day

GLEN ISLA

All over Scotland you'll find place names with the prefixes 'strath' and 'glen', like Strathclyde, Strathpeffer, Glencoe and Glentrool. Both words are Celtic in origin, and both mean 'valley', but that's where the similarity ends.

Straths are wide and flat, while glens are narrow and deep. To see the difference at first hand, head for the old county of Angus, just north of Dundee. Here Strathmore, running roughly from Perth up to Stonehaven, boasts some of Scotland's most productive arable farmland, most famous for its fields of berries. Yet, the north side of this 'garden of Scotland' forms the foothills of the Cairngorms; wild, moorland country penetrated by the Angus Glens. In order to explore most of the glens, walking boots are required. Eek! Thankfully, a handful are accessible to motor vehicles and reach from Strathmore into the mountains, like fingers on a hand.

We're setting off from 'the fair city' of Perth along the wonderful A93, passing Scone Palace, through Blairgowrie, and heading north until we can turn into Glen Isla. This is the most westerly of the Angus Glens and the only one that

allows us to ride right through. The road carries us south east, towards Kirriemuir from where we work our way along the line of glens. Glen Prosen is rather overshadowed by its more dramatic neighbours, but it's a delightful loop with fine views out over the glen particularly as we leave along the eastern hillside. The exit is marked by a roadside memorial to Captain Robert Scott and Edward Wilson. Dr Wilson lived in Glen Prosen for a while and Scott often joined him to prepare for their ill-fated trip to the South Pole in 1912. Now we're heading up the gorgeous B955 into Glen Clova, arguably the best known and most popular of the glens. It will probably be busier, with an unofficial one-way system operating on the single track road – if everyone travels in a clockwise direction, they should complete the circuit without meeting another vehicle. The further into Glen Clova you go, the steeper the hills and the more majestic

the landscape. After a loop down the other side of the water, we're back in Strathmore, passing to the north of Brechin until we can turn into Glen Esk. This long and captivating road ends at the head of the glen – or at least where Glen Esk divides to become Glen Lee and Glen Mark. The prize for making it this far is the impressively tall Invermark Castle, almost hidden by trees as you approach the end of the public road. Okay, it's a ruin and we're not allowed in, but it's still a mighty tower house in a splendid setting.

Once we're back on the 'main' road, it's very tempting to head for Fettercairn and over the B974 Cairn O' Mount road to Deeside. It's a great road, but it makes for a long day, so we're turning south, past the old Edzell air station to Montrose. Now we cut back inland, through Forfar to Glamis Castle, where the old Queen Mum was born. It's a picturesque castle but, in the eyes

of this beholder, it's got more conical turrets and towers than any single castle requires. With a quick stop in Forfar for a bridie, we head home through the lush farming countryside of Strathmore to Coupar Angus, Scone and back to Perth.

SOUNDTRACK

Ride On by AC/DC. Bon Scott, who provides the vocals on this track, was born in Forfar. Alternatively, although no more upbeat, *The Norland Wind* by Jim Reid. Dundee-born Reid put the music to *The Wild Geese*, a poem by Violet Jacob, who's buried in Kirriemuir.

FURTHER READING

Flemington and Tales From Angus by Violet Jacob (Cannongate, 2011). Ignore the truly dreadful cover and enjoy the book. Jacob was born near Montrose and gave up writing novels after her only son was killed at the Somme. Her poems – often tinged with sadness – are just as good.

GLEN CLOVA

1 Leave Perth on the A93 to Blairgowrie (15 miles)

2 After crossing the river, turn left on A93, signed Braemar, to road junction (14 miles)

3 Turn right onto B951, to Glenisla, and follow the road past Loch of Lintrathen to Kirkton of Kingoldrum (16 miles)

4 Turn left, as the main road bends round to the right, to crossroads (0.7 miles)

5 Turn right (unsigned) and follow the road to T-junction (2 miles)

6 Turn left and then right, following signs to Pearsie to T-junction (1 mile)

7 At the complicated T-junction, turn left to Prosen and follow signs to Glen Prosen (5 miles)

8 Soon after the road joins the river bank, turn right over a bridge, and right again following signs for Kirriemuir to T-junction at Dykehead (5 miles)

9 Turn left onto B955 to Clova (10 miles) (At the Clova Hotel, a left turn leads to the Ranger Station if you want to go to the head of the glen)

10 Turn right in front of the hotel, following the B955 back to Dykehead (10 miles)

11 Soon after Dykehead, fork left to reach a T-junction (0.5 miles)

12 Turn left through Cortachy to Memus (3 miles)

13 Turn left by the church, signed Glenogil, to pick up and follow signs to Edzell (13 miles)

14 In Edzell, turn left onto B966, signed Fettercairn (1.5 miles)

15 After crossing the river, turn left to Glen Esk (15 miles)

16 Return to B966 junction (15 miles)

17 Turn left for 400 yards, then right onto 'the lang straight', signed Northwaterbridge, to T-junction (4 miles)

18 Turn right onto A90 (dual carriageway), signed Forfar (600 yards)

19 Turn left to Hillside (5 miles)

20 At T-junction, turn right onto A937 to Montrose and follow signs for A92 Arbroath to lead through town centre, across the estuary and over the roundabout (3 miles)

21 Soon after the roundabout, turn right onto A934 and follow signs to Forfar, to the town centre (16 miles)

22 Continue through High Street to pick up and follow signs to A94 Coupar Angus (17 miles)

23 Continue to follow A94 back to Perth (13 miles)

Mount Battock
778

Glas Tulaichean
1051

Cairn of Claise
933

The Cairnwell
1062

Glen Glas

Devil's Elbow

CAIRNGORMS NATIONAL PARK

A93

Driesh
947

Clova

Glen Clova

Rottal

Spittal of Glenshee

Glen Prosen Village

Glen Prosen

Glen Isla

Glen Shee

Lair

B951

Kirkton of Glenisla

Dykehead

Finavon

Glen Esk

Water of Mark

Invermark Castle

Cairncross

Loch Lee

River N Esk

Gannochy

Cairn O' Mount

Clatterin Brig

Auchmull

Fettercairn

B974

B966

B967

Inverbervie

Laurencekirk

Edzell

A90

Marykirk

A937

St. Cyrus

Brechin

Hillside

B974

A120

Kirkmichael

A924

River Isla

Bridge of Cally

Alyth

B951

Kirkton of Kingoldrum

B967

Kirriemuir

A926

Loch Lintrathen

Forfar

A932

B9134

B9113

A935

A934

Montrose

Scurdie Ness

Lunan Bay

Lang Craig

A92

A933

Letham

B965

B9128

Blairgowrie

A926

A94

Glamis

B9127

A923

Dunkeld

Birnam

A984

Rattray

Meigle

Newtyle

A928

A90

B954

Crombie

B961

B978

Craigton

The Deil's Heid

Arbroath

Meikleour

Bankfoot

B869

A93

A94

Leys

A923

DUNDEE

A92

A930

Carnoustie

A9

Guildtown

Abernyte

Balbeggie

START

Old Scone

Scone

PERTH

A90

Invergowrie

Newport-on-Tay

Tayport

Tentsmuir Forest

A914

Monifieth

Buddon Ness

Firth of Tay

Fife

Cupar Angus

0   10 kms
0   5 miles

WHAT TO SEE

Montrose Air Station Heritage Centre (DD10 9BD). Britain's first military airfield was sited nearby in 1913 allowing the Royal Flying Corps to protect naval bases at Rosyth, Cromarty and Scapa Flow. The Centre is full of interest, including a replica of the Spitfire that the people of Arbroath funded to help the war effort.

Piper's Knoll (DD8 4QP) is a wonderful graveyard hidden among trees at the entrance to Glen Clova. The short access track is signposted off the B955, half a mile north of Dykehead (direction No.10 above). Quiet and secluded, it's not a bad place to be laid to rest.

LOOK OUT FOR

The Meikleour Beech Hedge (PH2 6DY) beside the A93 south of Blairgowrie. Planted in 1745, it's said to be the highest hedge in the world. It's trimmed and measured every ten years.

WHERE TO STAY

The Glen Clova Hotel (DD8 4QS) might be a bit pricey for the average biker's overnight, but don't rule out the **Climbers Bunkhouse** round the back. Refurbished for 2018, it's smarter than many hotels. No longer self-catering, but the hotel is just across the yard.

Druminoch B&B (DD8 5HD) near Kirkton of Kingoldrum is as peaceful as you'll find. Evening meals by prior arrangement.

WHERE TO EAT

Nip into Brechin where you'll be well fed at the **Auld Bakehouse** (DD9 6ER). Arbroath Smokies and Croque Madames on the same menu. Well worth the detour.

In Montrose, seek out the **Pavilion Cafe** (DD10 8HG) close to Montrose Academy. Great food, welcoming staff, nice atmosphere and perhaps a game of bowls to watch while you wait.

ARDNAMURCHAN AND THE ROAD TO THE ISLES

| TWISTY | STRAIGHTER |
| SINGLE TRACK | WIDER |

DISTANCE
170 miles

ALLOW
6 hours

LOCH NAN UAMH

In theory, the A82 beside Loch Linnhe should be terrific, but it's not!

Heavy traffic, 40mph speed limits and what seems like a never-ending, ten-mile double white line combine to spoil the fun. That's why the little Corran Ferry is such a joy, allowing us to opt out of the A82 convoy by boarding a little squint-loading ferry to Ardgour. A five minute crossing and we're set free on the empty roads we've come for.

We first head south with Loch Linnhe on our left before turning inland through the steep-sided Glen Tarbet to Strontian. From there, the road narrows and winds through ancient woodlands by Loch Sunart to Salen where we branch left. Now we're heading west, with blind summits, teasing bends and glorious views. After Glenborrodale we turn inland on a narrow road cut into the hillside far above the bay, with Mull out across the water. It's just a twisting thread of tarmac across a vast and gloriously empty peninsular until we arrive at traffic lights which control access to the lighthouse. We've arrived; as far west as it is possible to travel on the British mainland.

On your way back, top up your fuel at Kilchoan if you're running short

(it's 50 miles to the next pump) then head for Salen. Soon you're enjoying a wider road, for a while at least, that weaves – sometimes single track, sometimes not – through Acharacle to Kinlochmoidart. Look out for the sign to Doirlinn (after Acharacle) which offers a short detour to Castle Tioram, one of Scotland's most wonderful ruins. The setting is as magnificent as the building. This is the Rough Bounds, a region argued over between Vikings and Scots, staunchly Jacobite in Charlie's day and a wilderness through the ages. A good road carries us speedily and entertainingly to Lochailort, flowing bends and postcard views along the way. And if you think that's fun, wait until you turn towards Mallaig. This was single track for longer than the locals care to remember, the last section only upgraded in 2009. They waited a long time to wave goodbye to passing places, but the road they now have is an absolute belter. It's difficult not to

feel unleashed as you climb, twist and power your way up from the shoreline for the utterly gorgeous road to the isles. At Arisaig, there's a lovely six mile twisty section through Bridge of Keppoch which takes us past the Silver Sands of Morar – a string of picturesque beaches dotted along the coastline – before we rejoin the main road into Mallaig. Unless you're taking a ferry from Mallaig, you have to retrace your steps for a while but, goodness gracious me, who cares?

Back in Lochailort, it's a left turn and the fun continues along to Glenfinnan, initially made famous when Bonnie Prince Charlie kicked off the Jacobite rebellion there in 1745. Centuries later it gained further prominence when the viaduct achieved a minor – but tourist-attracting – role in the Harry Potter films. Now we're homeward bound by following the main road into Fort William and south to Ballachulish. Alternatively,

you may prefer to keep west of Loch Linnhe to return over the Corran Ferry and avoid the traffic south of Fort William. When you get back to the bridge at Ballachulish, you can extend your day by taking a turn around Loch Leven. Before the bridge was built, you either had to queue for the ferry or go round by Kinlochleven. In those days it was a pain, now it's a pleasure!

SOUNDTRACK

It's a long way to Ardnamurchan Point so you'll need two tracks. Firstly, *Keep Right on To The End Of The Road* by Sir Harry Lauder, then follow it up with Martyn Bennett's *Harry's in Heaven*. Compare and contrast.

FURTHER READING

Spade Among The Rushes by Margaret Leigh (Birlinn, 1996). One woman's struggle to transform a deserted croft into a home, and to claw land back from the wilderness.

THE ROAD TO ARDNAMURCHAN

WHAT TO SEE

Glenfinnan (PH37 4LT), where there's a lot to take in, including the 21-arched Glenfinnan viaduct that will be familiar to Harry Potter fans. The Jacobite steam train crosses it en route between Fort William and Mallaig – it's a fine sight if you time it right. The West Highland Railway Museum in the restored Glenfinnan station building is also worth a look. And down on the shore of Loch Shiel you'll find the towering Jacobite Monument, with a kilted Highlander at the top.

LOOK OUT FOR

A right turn in Strontian (PH36 4BB). If you feel like exploring, there's a tempting detour on a single track road over the hills, passing long-exhausted lead mines and down to Loch Doilet and the forestry village of Polloch. A forestry road leads through to Glenfinnan but you're not supposed to take motorcycles on it! There's another detour on the way to Ardnamurchan to a truly wonderful beach at **Sanna** (PH36 4LW).

WHERE TO STAY

The Fishermen's Mission Bunkhouse (PH41 4PY) in Mallaig offers private rooms and dormitories, is spotlessly clean and remarkably cheap. And whatever you spend supports a good cause. Breakfast is served in the Mission's café for an additional cost.

If you prefer a more traditional B&B, **Glencairn** is only a couple of minutes from the ferry terminal, and has a lovely view out over the harbour.

WHERE TO EAT

The Cabin (PH41 4PU) in Mallaig can get busy – and that's because it's good. Specialising in seafood, and you can either eat on the premises or take it away. There's a café in the **Kilchoan Community Centre** (PH36 4LJ) serving home bakes, filled roads, soup, etc. All profits help the local community. The **Glenfinnan Dining Car** (PH37 4LT) is fun, and close to the Harry Potter viaduct. It's a soup 'n' sandwich sort of a place where the train carriage surroundings are as important as the menu.

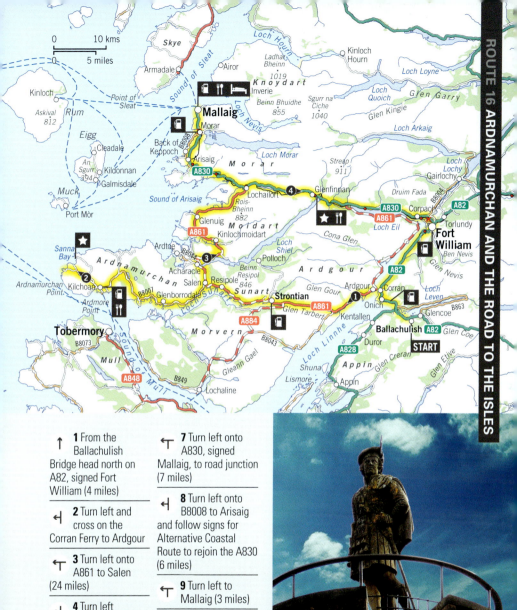

1 From the Ballachulish Bridge head north on A82, signed Fort William (4 miles)

2 Turn left and cross on the Corran Ferry to Ardgour

3 Turn left onto A861 to Salen (24 miles)

4 Turn left onto B8007 to Ardnamurchan (25 miles)

5 Return on B8007 to Salen (25 miles)

6 Turn left onto A861 to Lochailort (21 miles)

7 Turn left onto A830, signed Mallaig, to road junction (7 miles)

8 Turn left onto B8008 to Arisaig and follow signs for Alternative Coastal Route to rejoin the A830 (6 miles)

9 Turn left to Mallaig (3 miles)

10 Return on A830 to Lochailort and follow signs to A82 Fort William (42 miles)

11 Continue on A82 to Ballachulish (13 miles)

GLENFINNAN

AROUND THE CAIRNGORMS

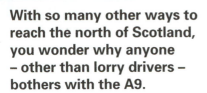

| TWISTY | STRAIGHTER |
| SINGLE TRACK | WIDER |

DISTANCE 160 miles

ALLOW 4.5 hours

THE LECHT

With so many other ways to reach the north of Scotland, you wonder why anyone – other than lorry drivers – bothers with the A9.

From Perth to Inverness, it's a summer-long, ulcer-inducing convoy, nose to tail, mile after mile waiting for the occasional stretch of dual carriageway for the mad dash until the road narrows again. Far better to head up the other side of the Cairngorm National Park, on the wonderful A93. If ever a road might have been put down for the pleasure of the motorcyclist, this is it.

The starting point at Pitlochry is easily – and enjoyably – reached from the south through Crieff and Aberfeldy. Pitlochry is full of people with selfie-sticks and shops selling tartan and shortbread, but head up to the more historic community of Moulin and immediately we're free of the crowds and powering our way up a series of bends onto the moor. A few miles further we turn north onto the beguiling A93 for an undulating and twisting run up the valley – brilliant fun whether you're on a laid-back cruiser or a stoked-up sports bike. Be careful, though – the A93 has a tendency of catching out the unwary and unwise, which is why there are regular signs warning bikers of the dangers ahead.

The bends are behind us as we approach Spittal of Glenshee, and from there it's an open, well-surfaced charge past the Glenshee Ski Centre, through the Cairnwell Pass (the highest main road in the UK). The good surface and languid curves continue down the other side heading for Braemar. Look out for a stone bridge on your left that carries the old military road over Clunie Water and offers an alternative route into the village if you feel like a change of pace.

Now we're running beside the River Dee to Crathie, where Deeside earns its Royal prefix – Balmoral Castle is hiding in the trees on the other side of the river. A left takes us back onto the high ground to Gairnsheil, over the hump-back bridge (built in 1751) to Cock Bridge. It's a steep climb round sharp corners as we set off for Tomintoul. The "A939 Cock Bridge

to Tomintoul" is always first in line when it comes to road closures due to snow, and it's easy to see why. The moorland is bleak, the winds often strong and the road defiantly strikes out across the heather apparently heading for the summit, although you go over the crest between hilltops at The Lecht ski station, this time on Scotland's second-highest road. Then it's down the other side in much the same manner, high gears all the way to Tomintoul. Apart from a few enjoyable and picturesque twists around Bridge of Brown, it's an easy and relaxing run to Grantown-on-Spey.

The simplest way back to Pitlochry is just to join the traffic on the A9, but it's almost as quick and a lot more fun to use the back roads as much as possible. It's a good, wide surface through Aviemore and along beside the Spey,

never very far from the A9 but often making better progress than the traffic on it. After Dalwhinnie we have to join the main road for 20 minutes until we can get back onto the 'old A9' that weaves its way through Blair Atholl and Killiecrankie to Pitlochry.

SOUNDTRACK

Caledonia by Dougie MacLean. Frankie Miller's version is terrific, as is Amy Macdonald's

FURTHER READING

The Living Mountain by Nan Shepherd (Canongate, 2011). A meditation on the Cairngorms, written during the Second World War but only published in 1977, a few years before the author died.

If you want to know what she looked like, she's been featuring on the Royal Bank of Scotland's £5 notes since 2016.

DIRECTIONS | AROUND THE CAIRNGORMS

1 In Pitlochry's main street, put Fishers Hotel on your left and turn right, signed Moulin and Braemar, to Kirkmichael (12 miles)

2 Soon after Kirkmichael, turn left onto B950 and follow signs to A93 Braemar (28 miles)

3 Continue ahead on A93 to a turn-off to Tomintoul, just before Crathie (9 miles)

4 Turn left onto B796 and follow signs to A939 Tomintoul (23 miles)

5 At T-junction on main street, turn right and follow signs to Grantown-on-Spey (14 miles)

6 At T-junction on main street, turn left, signed Inverness, to roundabout (0.5 miles)

7 Go right on roundabout to join A95 to Aviemore (13 miles)

8 Continue through Aviemore and follow B9152 to Kingussie and on to Newtonmore (15 miles)

9 At far end of the main street, bear right onto A86, signed Spean Bridge, to Laggan (8 miles)

10 Soon after the A86 crosses the River Spey, turn left onto A889, through Dalwhinnie to T-junction (9 miles)

11 Turn right onto A9 to the House of Bruar turn-off (19 miles)

12 Turn left onto B8079, through Blair Atholl and Killiecrankie to Pitlochry (10 miles)

WHAT TO SEE

Doughty bridges built for the military around 1750 and still carrying traffic today. There's one in Spittal of Glenshee (PH10 7QF), another on the approach to Braemar (AB35 5XS) and the much-photographed bridge at Gairnshiel (AB35 5UR) as we join the A939. The most spectacular of them all, but not open to vehicles any more, is the Old Bridge of Dee between Braemar and Crathie (AB35 5XQ) – six different-sized arches and a single humped-backed profile! We might still be using that bridge if Queen Victoria hadn't bought Balmoral, just downriver; the road was diverted and the new bridge built to ensure the Queen's privacy and security.

LOOK OUT FOR

'The Devil's Elbow' (PH10 7QQ), on the old road as you climb the valley towards Glenshee. The infamous double-hairpin bends have been by-passed by the A93, but you can still see the lower bend below you on the right-hand side, with the upper bend now part of the modern road. There's a line of wartime anti-tank blocks nearby.

WHERE TO STAY

Silverhowe B&B (PH16 5LY) in Pitlochry. Biker owned and biker friendly. **Parkburn Guest House** (PH26 3EN) in Grantown-on-Spey is a short walk from the centre of town, with comfy rooms and decent prices.

WHERE TO EAT

The Hungry Highlander (AB35 5YP) in Braemar usually has a bike or two outside it. A top-notch chip shop with limited seating but friendly service.

High Street Merchants (PH26 3EL) in Grantown-on-Spey is a classy café with a good menu and friendly staff.

Route 7 Café is in the Highland Homeware Centre (PH22 1ST), on an industrial estate off Dalfaber Drive. Hard to find, but the food is good and it's priced to attract the locals. If you don't mind paying more, **MacDui's** (PH22 1RH) by the station has a tie-in with Indian Motorcycles and the bar is has been themed accordingly.

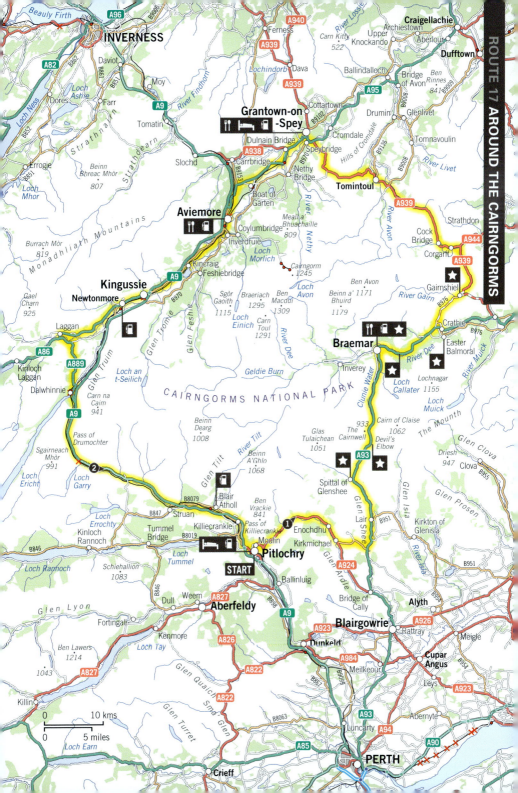

THE GREAT GLEN

TWISTY — **STRAIGHTER**	**DISTANCE** 140 miles
SINGLE TRACK — **WIDER**	**ALLOW** 4 hours

LOCH TARFF

You have to wonder where Thomas Telford found the time.

The 18th century stonemason turned self-taught architect and civil engineer built so many roads, bridges, harbours and canals it's hard to avoid them if you travel in the UK. He also found time to knock up a couple of dozen churches in the Highlands and Islands, a new town in Caithness and even helped with a country-crossing canal for the King of Sweden. When he died in 1834, probably of exhaustion, he was buried in Westminster Abbey. While almost everything he created is still in use today, he is something of a forgotten man – certainly when compared to the cigar-smoking, top-hat wearing johnny-come-lately Brunel.

As motorcyclists, we should all get down on our knees and thank the Lord for giving us little Tam Telford, the shepherd's son from Eskdale in Dumfriesshire. He created over a thousand miles of roads in Scotland, opening routes that we still follow today. In fact, many of the best biking roads follow Telford's routes. Among them is the A82 from Glasgow to Inverness, which runs up Loch Lomondside, through Glencoe to Inverness, close to another of his masterpieces – the Caledonian Canal.

By the time the canal was completed in 1822, circumstances conspired to make it unnecessary and Telford regarded it as a waste of his time. Nevertheless, the scale of the engineering and the beauty of the construction make it one of the great marvels of the 19th century.

Telford is our companion as we set out from Spean Bridge along his A82 south to the outskirts of Fort William. We then head back north on the other side of the valley, beside Neptune's Staircase – the longest staircase lock in Britain – on the Caledonian Canal. As we shadow the canal to Loch Lochy, be prepared for the incongruous sight of a boat apparently sailing through the countryside. (There's a dead-end detour to Loch Arkaig if you want to extend your outing. Turn left just before crossing the canal and follow the signs. It's 18 narrow miles to the far end before you have to come

back.) Then we cross back to the A82 before heading to Fort Augustus and Loch Ness. The loch itself is, like Fort William, distinctly underwhelming. It's like the Kardashians – famous, but it's hard to work out why. It's big but lacking in drama; you can't see much for trees, the roads tends to be busy and the villages are hoaching with visitors. So having ticked Loch Ness off our 'seen that' list, we can turn inland at Drumnadrochit to a (roughly) parallel road that takes us north through lovely country without the need to follow a lorry along miles of double white lines. As we ride into Inverness along the Beauly Firth, stop at Clachnaharry to admire how Telford's team solved the problem of shallow water where the canal met the sea. They simply built a peninsula out to deeper water, then put a canal up the middle of it. Genius! A few miles of A9 dual carriageway

takes us down to Daviot, where we cut back south west into farming country untouched by tourism. Expect single track roads, scattered housing and glorious views all the way to Fort Augustus, where Telford's road will lead us back to Spean Bridge.

↑ **1** From Spean Bridge, take the A82 south towards Fort William (7 miles)

↻ **2** At roundabout by Ben Nevis Distillery, turn right onto A830 to cross canal (1 mile)

↦ **3** Turn right into B8004, signed Gairlochy, to the Commando Memorial (9 miles)

↰ **4** Turn left onto A82, signed Inverness, to Drumnadrochit (40 miles)

↰ **5** Just over the bridge, turn left onto A831 (1 mile)

↦ **6** Turn right onto A833, signed Beauly, to T-junction (10 miles)

↱ **7** Turn left onto A862 to Inverness (10 miles)

↑ **8** Leave Inverness by the A9 (southbound), signed Perth (8 miles)

↦ **9** Turn right (crossing the other carriageway) onto B851 to Fort Augustus (31 miles)

↰ **10** Turn left onto A82 back to Spean Bridge (22 miles)

WHAT TO SEE

The Commando Memorial (PH34 4EG) at Spean Bridge. The Commando's training base was at Achnacarry Castle, some six miles away, and new recruits – all volunteers – marched from Spean Bridge station to the castle, passing the spot where the memorial now stands. It's a moving tribute in a spectacular location.

Urquhart Castle (IV63 6XJ) sits on a headland overlooking Loch Ness just before Drumnadrochit. These impressive ruins date from the 13th century and the castle was fought over almost constantly until the 18th century, when it was destroyed to stop it being used by Jacobites. It's now one of the most visited castles in Scotland.

LOOK OUT FOR

Nessie?

Failing that, keep an eye out for the **memorial to John Cobb** (IV63 6XJ), who died on Loch Ness as he attempted to break the world speed record on water in 1952. The bullet-shaped cairn sits at the roadside about nine miles north of Invermoriston, but trees screen the view to the water. He deserves better.

WHERE TO STAY

Park Guest House (IV3 5PB) in Inverness has been around a long time, so they know how to make you feel welcome. Big rooms, big breakfast, a brisk ten-minute walk from the centre of town.

WHERE TO EAT

Thistle Stop Café (PH35 4HN) at Abercalder, midway between Invergarry and Fort Augustus. A straightforward café and shop offering value for money and friendly service. The section of car park nearest the entrance has been surfaced and reserved for motorbikes. Quite right too!

Café Eighty2 (IV63 6UL) at Lewiston, as you approach Drumnadrochit. The rather plain exterior hides a cosy, quirky café with varied food and friendly service. It's just past the petrol station on the right-hand side.

Café V8 (IV1 1SN) is a truck stop in the industrial quarter of Inverness. The food is filling, the prices are cheap, and there's plenty of space to park.

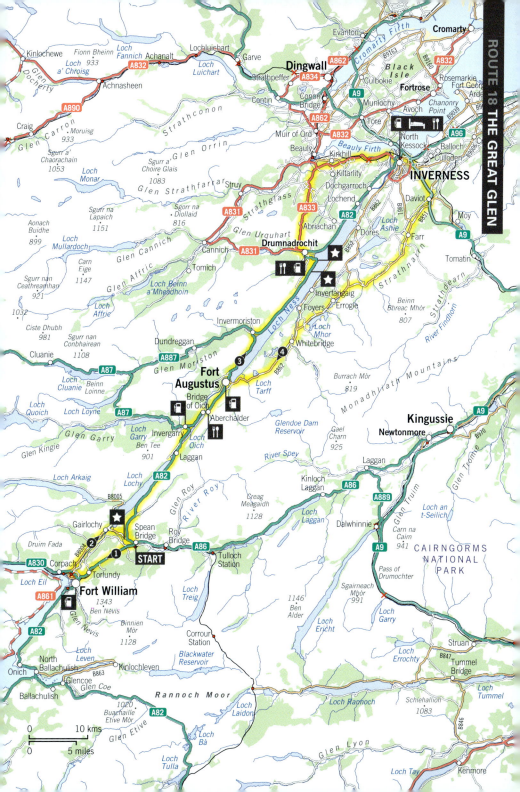

ROUTE 19
THE WESTERN ISLES

TWISTY ▮▬▬ STRAIGHTER	📍 **DISTANCE** 207 miles
SINGLE TRACK ▮▬▬ WIDER	🕐 **ALLOW** 2+ days

'THE GOLDEN ROAD', HARRIS

Only 40 miles separate the Western Isles from the Scottish mainland, but the two could hardly be more different.

For a start, there's the mother tongue – in the Western Isles, many people speak Gaelic (that's 'Gallic', by the way, not 'Gay-lick') as their first language. The road signs are predominantly in Gaelic as well. Then there's religion – staunchly Catholic in the south and strongly Protestant in the north. The Lord's Day is still observed in Lewis and Harris and many businesses and facilities remain closed on Sundays. The rock from which the islands are formed dates from the creation of the earth itself, the landscape varies from barren mountain to fertile pasture and the coastline is fringed with everything from jagged rock to spotless white sands. Almost all the main islands are speckled by lochs and lochans – over 6000, at the last count. The Western Isles might be part of Scotland, but they feel like a different world.

Ferries from Ullapool, Skye or Oban will deliver you to the north, middle or south of the chain of islands respectively. Internal ferries and causeways make it simple to travel from top to bottom or vice versa. Let's face it, if you're

coming this far, it's a shame not to see as many islands as possible, so we suggest sailing from Oban to Barra in the south. The boat arrives in time to explore this small but delightful island during the evening. Next day, cross to Eriskay, where the SS *Politician* – of 'Whisky Galore' fame – ran aground in 1941. We pass the beach where Bonnie Prince Charlie landed on his way to his disastrous defeat at Culloden in 1745, before heading over the causeway to South Uist. The rich, sandy grassland – machair – which is only found on west coasts carries us north. The first causeway takes us over a loch, the next over tidal sands to Benbecula. It is an extraordinary landscape, peppered with lochs, lochans and glorified puddles. We skip from causeway to causeway, hardly able to tell what's land and what's sea. A few hundred yards on Grimsay and we're over onto North Uist and, after

some more glorious miles, to the ferry from Berneray to Leverburgh.

As we arrive in Harris, we turn east to the unclassified 'Golden Road', so-called because of the cost of construction. It links the scattered coastal communities between Rodel and Tarbert, twisting and turning throughout, with unforgiving verges if you make a mistake. Use your gears, take your time and marvel at both the landscape and the commitment of the road builders. It's magical! When you rejoin the highway short of Tarbert, it's worth heading left for a few miles to see the sublime white beaches along Harris's western shoreline before continuing north. In North Harris and Lewis, the road is more conventional but the views no less spectacular as we make for the Callanish Stones (Scotland's Stonehenge), a village of 'blackhouses' at Gearrannan and finally the northernmost tip of the Hebrides.

Listeners to the shipping forecast will be familiar with the Butt of Lewis, but it usually raises a chuckle when people come across it for the first time. If that's you, you'll probably laugh out loud when you see the sign for 'Butt View Stores'. How you return home depends on your plans hereafter; Stornoway offers a ferry to Ullapool or you could head back to Tarbert for a shorter crossing to Skye.

SOUNDTRACK

The Heb Celt Bounce by Face the West. What better than a bit of piping/rock for a trip to the Outer Hebs?

FURTHER READING

Everyday Gaelic by Morag Macneill (Birlinn, 2015). Teach yourself to speak like a local, with a CD to help you sound authentic. Good luck.

1 From Castlebay Ferry terminal, Barra:

⬅ **2** Head left onto A888 to Northbay (6 miles)

⬅ **3** Turn right, signed Ferry & Airport, to ferry terminal (2 miles)

⬅ **4** Take the ferry to Eriskay

⬆ **5** Follow signs to South Uist and cross the causeway to join A888 to Daliburgh (10 miles)

⬅ **6** Turn left onto A865 to North Uist, picking up signs to Sound of HarrisFerry (57 miles)

⬅ **7** Take the ferry to Leverburgh

➡ **8** Turn right to A859, signed Tarbert, to T-junction (0.5 mile)

➡ **9** Turn right onto A859, signed Roghadal, to join 'The Golden Road' to T-junction (14 miles)

➡ **10** Turn right onto A859, through Tarbert, to junction with brown tourism signs for Callanish Stones (33 miles)

⬅ **11** Turn left to join A858, passing Callanish Stones (9 miles) and the sign to Gearrannan (7 miles beyond) to T-junction (28 miles)

⬅ **12** Turn left onto A857 to Port of Ness (15 miles)

⬅ **13** Turn left onto B8013, signed Eoropaidh, to the Butt of Lewis (2 miles)

⬇ **14** From the Butt of Lewis to Stornoway, follow signs to Steornabhagh (29 miles)

WHAT TO SEE

From Barra cross the causeway to Vatersay and bear left. After two miles you'll find the remains of a **Catalina Flying Boat** (HS5 9YN) that crashed on the hillside in 1944.

It doesn't cost much to get out to **Kisimul Castle** (HS9 5UZ) in Castlebay, and it's surprisingly cosy inside (in a sort of "Blimey! This must have been grim in the old days" kind of a way).

There's a life-sized statue of **Hercules the Bear** on North Uist that now marks his grave. Hercules was a Grizzly who was the pet/friend/co-star of the wrestler Andy Robin. In 1980 he enjoyed three weeks of freedom after escaping from a film shoot in the area. After his death in 2000, it was decided that he should be laid to rest in Langass Woods (HS6 5HA), on the right as you head west towards Lochmaddy.

There are the **standing stones** at Callanish (HS2 9DY), the restored **Blackhouse village** (HS2 9AL) at Gearrannan mentioned above and the **Blackhouse Museum** along the road at Arnol (HS2 9BD). The museum offers a great insight into the old way of life for the locals, although those days are not nearly as 'old' as you might expect.

LOOK OUT FOR

Dolphins swimming beside the inter-island ferries. Keep a lookout around the bow.

WHERE TO STAY

Endeavour (HD9 5XD) in Castlebay. It's small, comfy and very friendly, with bedrooms looking out to Kisimul Castle. What a way to start your visit.

If you fancy a night in a modernised blackhouse, book into the **Gearrannan Hostel** (HS2 9AL). Hard to beat for atmosphere.

In Stornoway, the **Tower Guest House** (HS1 2QN) has good rates and even offers single rooms.

WHERE TO EAT

Café Kisimul (HS9 5XD) in Castlebay serves all day and offers a menu specialising in Indian, Italian or local seafood.

If you're waiting for the ferry at Berneray, the **Lobster Pot Tearoom** (HS6 5BJ) is close to the ferry ramp and does a good soup and sandwich.

Eleven Restaurant & Bar (HS1 2QN) is a popular place to eat in Stornoway offering a 'help yourself' buffet, discounts for eating early, etc. There are loads of tables, but it does get busy.

0   10 kms
0   5 miles

Butt of Lewis
Port of Ness
A857
Borve
Lewis
Muirneag 248
Barvas
Tolsta Head
A858
A857
Great Bernera
Carloway
Beinn Mholach 291
Tiumpan Head
Timsgearraidh
Broad Bay
Callanish
Eye Peninsula
B8011
A858
A859
Stornoway
Leurbost
B8060
A859
Scarp
North Harris
Hushinish
Clisham 799
Shiant Isles
The Minch
Loch a Siar
B887
Taransay
Tarbert
Harris
Luskentyre
Scalpay
A859
Pabbay
Northton
Leverburgh
Sound of Harris
Berneray
Boreray
Renish Point
North Uist
A865
Monach Islands
A865
A867
Lochmaddy
Sound of Monach
A865
Balivanich
Grimsay
Benbecula
Wiay
South Uist
Howmore
Rubha Roiseal
Daliburgh
Lochboisdale
Sound of Barra
Eriskay
Barra
Northbay
Vatersay
Castlebay
START
Sandray
Pabbay
Sound of Pabbay
Mingulay
Berneray
Barra Head

The Little Minch
Rubha Hunish
Uig
Loch Dunvegan
Loch Snizort
A87
A855
Sound of Raasay
Rona
Dunvegan Head
A850
Neist
Dunvegan
Portree
Raasay
Inner Sound
A863
Loch Bracadale
Skye
A87
Broadford
A851
Soay
Canna
Rum
Mallaig
Eigg
Muck

Western Isles

The Minch

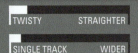

ROUTE 20
INVERGARRY TO SKYE

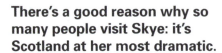

TWISTY	STRAIGHTER	**DISTANCE** 232 miles
SINGLE TRACK	WIDER	**ALLOW** 1 day

TROTTERNISH, SKYE

There's a good reason why so many people visit Skye: it's Scotland at her most dramatic.

It's a landscape of jagged mountains and craggy headlands, ruined castles and colourful villages, sparkling lochs and towering sea cliffs. The island is also rich in history, most of it painful – Jacobite uprisings, clan warfare and the Highland Clearances. It's a brilliant place! The trouble is that, in summer, Skye is mobbed! Cruise ships, coaches and camper vans are arriving in such numbers that Skye struggles to cope at the peak of the season. Lately, the police have even issued advice to people not to come to Skye unless they had pre-booked accommodation. To avoid the mayhem, visit during the spring or autumn, if you can. In spite of the crowds, Skye is magical, and this outing is magnificent.

The journey begins on the spectacular A87, although after five miles you might be tempted by a left turn, which leads along a 23-mile, unclassified road through wild, empty but spellbindingly beautiful countryside to Kinloch Hourn. There's nothing much at the far end apart from sea, solitude and a wee tearoom which closes when the owner is fetching supplies. But you won't regret the journey even when you're

retracing your route back to the A87. From Loch Garry, we climb the hillside to follow the contour round past Loch Loyne and then Loch Cluanie, with the impressive face of Ciste Dhubh (one of the Five Sisters of Kintail) ahead of us. The road is made up of long straights and sweeping curves, and the descent to Shiel Bridge is fabulous. Turn left here for the original and most enchanting route to Skye, over the soaring Mam Ratagan Pass to the last turntable ferry in the country. It's a steep climb of over 1,000 feet through trees until you burst into the open at the top. The views are superb to the Five Sisters, Loch Duich and ahead to the Sound of Sleat. Then it's down to Glenelg. If you have time (and it's worth making time) before catching the ferry, explore the little roads south of the village: Arnisdale is enchanting, and the two brochs (Pictish defensive towers) in Glenbeag are as good as you'll find anywhere.

Then let the ferry to Kylerhea carry you over the sea to Skye; manually-operated and community-run, it's worth the ticket price ten times over. But be warned, it's a cash only service. No cards!

Skye starts with the narrow Bealach Udal that carries us up from the slipway, clinging to the hillside as the peaks of the Cuillins slowly appear ahead. From the summit, Skye is laid out below and every corner is worthy of exploration: Sleat in the south offers the Clan Donald Centre and the atmospheric Dunscaith Castle ruins; you haven't really seen the Cuillins until you've viewed them from Elgol; nip down Glen Brittle to see the crystal-clear Fairy Pools; visit the seat of the Clan MacLeod at Dunvegan; and head round the top of Trotternish in the north of the island to the tragic Duntulm Castle. It was abandoned by the MacDonalds in the 18th century, apparently after the nursemaid dropped the clan chief's baby out of a window while looking at boats!

On the east coast of Trotternish, there's a most extraordinary landscape that seems to have come straight from the set of a Tolkein movie. As we head for home, wonderful views of mountains and sea lochs keep us company through Sligachan to the iconic Skye Bridge. From Kyle of Lochalsh, you can either set off for Applecross and the joys of the north-west, nip into Plockton or zip back to Invergarry, stopping off for the obligatory photo opportunity at Eilean Donan Castle on the way.

SOUNDTRACK

Obair Oidhche by Niteworks – a touch of Celtic electronica from the locals, fusing club beats, traditional instruments and Gaelic.

FURTHER READING

Cross Stitch by Diana Gabaldon (Arrow, 1992). Never heard of it? In the US, it was called *Outlander*. Fifty shades of tartan!

Note: The Glenelg/Kylerhea ferry only operates between Easter and October. And it only accepts cash.

↑ **1** From Invergarry (PH35 4HJ), take the A87, signed Kyle of Lochalsh, to Shiel Bridge (34 miles)

↰ **2** Turn left, signed Ratagan (and Glenelg Ferry) (9 miles)

↱ **3** Bear right at the fork, signed Galltair, to the ferry slipway (2 miles)

🚢 **4** Take the ferry

↑ **5** At Kylerhea, follow the road to T-junction (7 miles)

↰ **6** Turn left onto A87 to Portree (30 miles)

↑ **7** Continue through Portree onto A855 through Staffin (18 miles)

↰ **8** After Staffin, turn left, signed Quiraing, to junction (6 miles) **Note:** To visit Duntulm Castle, continue on the A855 for a further 7 miles. Return to this point to rejoin the route.

↰ **9** Turn left onto A855 to junction by Uig (1 mile)

↰ **10** Turn left onto A87 to Dunvegan turn off (11 miles)

↱ **11** Turn right onto A850 to Dunvegan (17 miles)

↰ **12** Turn left onto A863 to Sligachan (23 miles)

↱ **13** Turn right onto A87, crossing the Skye Bridge to Kyle of Lochalsh (25 miles)

14 Continue on A87 to Invergarry (49 miles)

WHAT TO SEE

The Quiraing (IV51 9LB) and **The Storr** (IV51 9HX). The first is a dramatic escarpment of land-slipped cliffs and pinnacles. You can see it from the road, but it's better close up. It's roughly a half-hour walk from the highest parking area on the road from Staffin to Uig. At The Storr, you'll see bizarre pinnacles of crumbling basalt including the most famous, The Old Man of Storr. It's about a mile from the car park if you want to get a closer look.

LOOK OUT FOR

Bernera Barracks (IV40 8JR) in Glenelg. They were built in the 1720s to control the crossing to Skye, as part of the Government's efforts to keep the lid on the Jacobite problem. The barracks have been ruined for 200 years but still make an imposing sight. They're in poor shape structurally, though, so don't go any closer than the perimeter fence.

Sea eagles from the Glenelg/Kylerhea ferry. They can often be spotted from the slipway or the boat as you cross, particularly on a rising tide when fish are most plentiful. A detour opportunity to **Neist Point**. About half a mile after Dunvegan, a right turn (signed to Glendale) marks the start of a 10 mile dead-end detour to the lighthouse at Neist Point. It's worth making the effort!

WHERE TO STAY

Generally speaking, avoid booking accommodation on Skye itself unless you're prepared to pay through the nose. Find somewhere on the mainland. An exception might be **Saucy Mary's** (IV41 8PH) in Kyleakin – it's very much at the cheap and cheerful end of the market, offering bunkhouse accommodation for groups, or twin rooms if you prefer. Breakfast is extra. Wherever you stay in this part of Scotland, book ahead!

WHERE TO EAT

Sheena's Tea Hut (IV40 8JH) is at the far end of the Corran road, through Glenelg and past Arnisdale. Just drive until the road stops and the hut is on your left. Lovely!

Café Arriba in Portree (IV51 9BD) is a safe bet for a hearty breakfast, filling lunch or a bistro dinner, although it's often pretty busy.

The Red Brick Café (IV51 9HL) is on an industrial estate just north of Portree, in a big shed with 'Jans' written on it. It's a modern eatery with a shop that sells everything from animal feed to socket sets, bathroom accessories to lawnmowers. Unlike most cafés on Skye, they'll also hire you a mini-digger.

Gairloch

Fionn Loch

Loch Maree

A832

A835

Sgurr 1093
Mor

Loch Fannich

B8056

Slioch
980

W e s t e r   R o s s

A832

Kinlochewe

A832

Achnasheen

T o r r i d o n

Beinn Eighe
1010

Torridon

Shieldaig

A896

Applecross

Loch Monar

A890

Strathcarron

Lochcarron

Loch Carron

A890

Loch Mullardoch

Cannich

Quiraing

Staffin

Trotternish

A855

A87

Uig

Loch Snizort

Dunvegan Head

Waternish

B886

B884

A850

Dunvegan

Neist

Duirinish

Macleod's Maidens

Loch Bracadale

A863

Struan

Bracadale

Drynoch

Skye

Loch Eynort

Cuillin Hills

B8083

Loch Brittle

Elgol

Soay

Sligachan

Portree

B883

2

3

Sconser

Scalpay

Raasay

Sound of Raasay

Rona

Inner Sound

Kyle of Lochalsh

Kyleakin

Broadford

A87

Kylerhea

Glenelg

Shiel Bridge

Arnisdale

Kinloch Hourn

Ladhar Bheinn

K n o y d a r t

1

4

Five Sisters

Glen Shiel

Kintail

Carn Eige

1147

Loch Affric

Invermo

River Moriston

Cluanie

Loch Cluanie

A87

A887

Fort Augustus

START

A87

Invergarry

Loch Quoich

River Garry

Loch Lochy

B8005

A82

Mallaig

A830

Loch Morar

Sound of Sleat

Ardvasar

A851

Sleat

Sound of Sleat

Sound of Canna

Canna

Rùm

Eigg

Sound of Rum

Loch Arkaig

Loch Eil

Spean Bridge

A86

River Farra

0   10 kms

0   5 miles

THE OLD BRIDGE, SLIGACHAN

ROUTE 21
SPEYSIDE TO BANFF

TWISTY	STRAIGHTER	
SINGLE TRACK	WIDER	

DISTANCE
155 miles

ALLOW
4 hours

CRAIGELLACHIE BRIDGE

The landscape of north-east Scotland may lack the drama of the Highlands, but don't let that put you off.

There's plenty of interest around this circuit, the traffic is refreshingly sparse and the roads are simply outstanding. Grantown-on-Spey was built by the local laird, Sir James Grant, in the late 18th century, to rehouse workers on his estate. With its long, grassy square, grey stone buildings and picturesque setting in the Spey Valley, it has been attracting visitors since Victorian times. The Spey is probably best known for whisky and fishing: anglers come from around the world – and pay handsomely – in the hope of catching a salmon on the river. And many of Scotland's finest whiskies are produced on Speyside before being sent around the globe.

Our route sounds like a roll call of famous malts as we set off to Tomintoul, passing through Knockandhu and Tomnavoulin on our way to Glenlivet, Aberlour and Craigellachie. Then we're in Dufftown – boasting no fewer than six working distilleries – and heading away from the Spey. Huntly is deftly by-passed via a short hop on a busy trunk road before we head north. Here the tarmac is wide and kind, allowing us to stay in top

gear as we cross the River Deveron to the 30mph limit at Aberchirder, known locally as 'Foggieloan', or just 'Foggie'. It's feels like it's just half a street wide, but Foggie has hidden depths – there's an impressively uniform 'planned' village behind the houses to your left. Then we're opening the throttle again to Banff. The main road leading west carries the traffic between Aberdeen and Inverness, so we're shadowing it by hopping along a series of charming coastal villages, built round the harbours

and facing resolutely out into the North Sea: Portsoy, Cullen, Portknockie, Findochty and Buckie. Further along, we reach Burghead, built on a grid like so many of the north-east villages. The harbour is Thomas Telford's work, as are the three warehouses that overlook it. Then it's across the main road and into Forres for the homeward leg. The trees give way to moorland, the views open up to the Cairngorms and the road obliges with every turn – a thrilling leg-stretcher back to Grantown-on-Spey.

SOUNDTRACK

I Wish I Were a Punk Rocker by Sandi Thom (She's fae Banff) or *Macpherson's Farewell* by Hamish Imlach (who wasnae).

FURTHER READING

The Testament of Gideon Mack by James Robertson (Penguin, 2007)

CROVIE, ABERDEENSHIRE

WHAT TO SEE

Don't pass this way without stopping to admire two lovely but very different bridges. Firstly **The Old Bridge of Livet** (AB37 9BT) is a twin-arched packhorse bridge in Glenlivet. It's roughly the same age and condition as the one in Carrbridge but this has two arches and is less well known. Then up the road in Craigellachie you'll find **Thomas Telford's bridge-building masterpiece** (IV32 7QJ). Cast iron, stone and two centuries old, it puts the nearby modern replacement to shame. And in Portknockie head for Addison Street (AB56 4NN) on the seafront and walk a couple of minutes along the headland – **Bow Fiddle Rock** is one of Scotland's most extraordinary rock formations.

You might also consider a spin along the coast to the east of Banff to see the little coastal communities at **Gardenstown, Crovie** and – the most famous of them all – **Pennan**, where Local Hero was filmed. Just follow the B9031 and look for the signs. Pennan, the farthest of the three, is 11 miles east of Banff.

LOOK OUT FOR

'**The Clock That Hanged MacPherson**' in the tower in Dufftown (AB55 4AL). In 1700, when the clock was housed in Banff, Lord Duff of Braco is said to have had the hands moved forward to ensure that Jamie MacPherson was hung before his pardon arrived. The story was immortalised in 'MacPherson's Farewell', the best-known version of which was written by Robert Burns (allegedly from MacPherson's own words).

WHERE TO STAY

The Sail Loft Bunkhouse (AB45 2RQ) in Portsoy shows how new life can be breathed into a ruined building. Beach-front location with private rooms or dorms. They'll provide meals by prior arrangement; you can use the kitchen to self-cater or walk into the town to a pub.

WHERE TO EAT

You can't come to Cullen without sampling the skink. **Lily's Kitchen** (AB56 4SH) makes a fine bowl of the smoked haddock soup and doesn't charge a fortune. A friendly wee caff.

1 From the traffic lights in Grantown-on Spey's Main Street, take the A939 and follow signs to Tomintoul (14 miles)

2 Turn left on A939, then ahead onto B9008 to T-junction (14 miles)

3 Turn right onto A95, signed Elgin (9 miles)

4 Just before Craigellachie, turn right onto A941 to Dufftown (5 miles)

5 At clocktower, turn left and follow signs to Huntly (13 miles)

6 At T-junction, turn right onto A96 (2 miles)

7 Turn left onto A97 to Banff (20 miles)

8 Turn left onto A98, signed Inverness, through Banff (2 miles)

9 Turn right onto B9038, signed Whitehills (500 yards)

10 Turn left onto B9139 Portsoy to T-junction (5 miles)

11 Turn right onto A98 through Cullen (6 miles)

12 Turn right onto A942 Portknockie through Findochty to Buckie and back to A98 (7 miles)

13 Turn right onto A98 to roundabout at Fochabers (6 miles)

14 Turn right onto A96, signed Forres (7 miles)

15 Just past Lhanbryde, turn right onto B9103 and follow signs to Lossiemouth (6 miles)

16 At the harbour, turn left onto B9040 to Burghead (8 miles)

17 When leaving Burghead, take first right onto B9089 to Kinloss (5 miles)

18 Continue ahead, crossing roundabout into Forres (2 miles)

19 At far end of High Street, turn left on the roundabout and follow signs back to Grantown-on-Spey A940/A939 (22 miles)

STRATHGLASS AND GLEN AFFRIC

TWISTY	STRAIGHTER	**DISTANCE** 75 miles
SINGLE TRACK	WIDER	**ALLOW** 3.5 hours

GLEN AFFRIC

Some of Scotland's most special places can be found up dead ends – roads that the unadventurous might regard as leading nowhere.

If you're put off by a 'No Through Road' sign, you'll never visit Ardnamurchan, for instance, or Crinan, or Achiltibuie or any number of wonderful places around the country. Glen Affric, a few miles west of Loch Ness, is another that more than repays the fact that you have to leave on the same road by which you arrived. To get there, we're taking the long way round, by gratefully turning off the busy highway along Loch Ness for a chest-thumping climb up past Abriachan. The road is narrow, twisting and steep, but once things level off we're snaking across open country, with the congestion of the A82 a fast-fading memory. Soon we're back onto an A road framed by rich farmland with the surface smooth and silky as we power north towards Beauly. Then we're heading south again, following the wide river valley of Strathglass to Cannich, where we arrive over a narrow bridge with traffic lights. The village is on a crossroads and we're taking each

road in turn. First, we head right into Glen Cannich, the road considerably shortened in 1952 when they flooded the valley for hydro-electricity. It's only nine miles before we have to turn back, but it's worth making the trip if only to see the massive concrete dam – some half-a-mile wide – that holds back Loch Mullardoch.

Back to Cannich, and another right turn allows us to join the road to Glen Affric, just past the power station at Fasnakyle. Glen Affric is where a perfect combination of mountain, loch and river forms one of Scotland's most beautiful glens. And with some magnificent Scots pine trees – the last

remnants of the ancient Caledonian Forest – as well as golden eagles, black grouse and pine martens, it can also claim to be among the most interesting. The single track road leads us along the shore of Loch Beinn a' Mheadhain and ends in a parking area close to Loch Affric, although you need to walk a short distance to enjoy the view into the upper reaches of the glen. Back in Cannich, we turn right again for the run back to Loch Ness, climbing onto moorland then dropping down the other side. It's a good road with plenty of engaging corners and enough straight sections to ensure we're rarely held up by traffic as we make our way through Glen Urquhart to Drumnadrochit. After

passing Nessieland (yes, honestly!), we arrive back at the A82. Turn left for Inverness, or right to Urquhart Castle and Fort William.

SOUNDTRACK

Urban: Rip the Calico by Red Hot Chilli Pipers. Not to be confused with the *Peppers*, this is a pipe band with attitude.

FURTHER READING

Isolation Shepherd by Iain R Thomson (Birlinn, 2016). The experiences of a young shepherd and his family in the remotest corner of remote Glen Strathfarrar, now submerged under a reservoir. A timeless account of a lost way of life.

PLODDA FALLS

WHAT TO SEE

Plodda Falls (IV4 7LY). When leaving Glen Affric, turn right, then right again to ride through the village of Tomich to a car park three miles beyond. It's two minutes on foot to a 'skywalk', which allows you to look down over the waterfall into a natural rock pool 40 metres below.

Urquhart Castle (IV63 6XJ) is a couple of miles south of Drumnadrochit, and occupies a magnificent position overlooking Loch Ness. It's easy to see why it's one of the most photographed castles in Scotland. (Entry fee)

LOOK OUT FOR

Eagles, **deer**, **otters**, **grouse**, **Scots pine**, **pine martens**, **Douglas fir**, etc, etc. And **cyclists** and **hillwalkers**.

WHERE TO STAY

Westward B&B (IV4 7LT) in Cannich. Comfortable, friendly, keenly priced and full of character. They'll dry your gear as well if needs be.

WHERE TO EAT

Corner on the Square (IV4 7BY) in Beauly. It's a mile off our route, but this little deli on the main street is worth going out of the way for.

Bog Cotton Café (IV4 7LN) in Cannich. Find it in the caravan park if you need a quick boost!

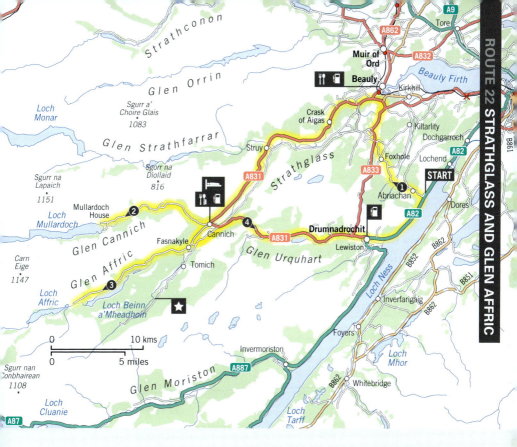

NOTE: The route starts on the A82, 8 miles south of Inverness and 6 miles north of Drumnadrochit (IV3 8LA). Turn off the A82, where it is signposted to Abriachan.

1 Take the unclassified road, climbing steeply to Abriachan (1.5 miles)

4 Bear left at fork, signed Foxhole, to T-junction (5 miles)

5 Turn right onto A833 to T-junction (2.5 miles)

6 Turn left onto A862, signed Beauly, to cross river (1 mile)

7 Bear left onto A831, signed Cannich (16 miles)

8 Turn right to Glen Cannich (9 miles)

9 Return to Cannich (9 miles)

10 Turn right, through the village to power station (2 miles)

11 Turn right to Glen Affric (9 miles)

12 Return to power station (7 miles) **Note:** Turn right and right again after 350 yards to visit Plodda Falls.

13 Turn right (leaving power station to your left) to T-junction (2 miles)

14 Turn right onto A831 to Drumnadrochit (11 miles)

15 Turn left for Inverness (15 miles) or right for Fort Augustus (19 miles)

ROUTE 23
NORTH COAST 500

TWISTY ▮▯ STRAIGHTER	📍 **DISTANCE** 514 miles
SINGLE TRACK ▮▯ WIDER	⏱ **ALLOW** 3 - 4 days

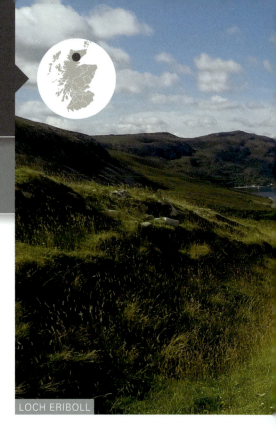

LOCH ERIBOLL

In just a few short years this glorious circuit round the top of Scotland has become one of the most famous touring routes on the planet.

No less an authority than *Condé Nast Traveller* suggested it "may be the best road trip in the world". Strange to think that, until 2015, the roads that snaked around the coastline of Ross & Cromarty, Sutherland and Caithness were all but deserted. We could all confidently head north anticipating traffic-free roads with only sheep, the occasional grey tractor or fish farm lorry to worry about. Not any more! Thanks to a clever concept and savvy marketing, the NC500 has attracted bikers, caravans, camper-vans, cars and classic cars to Britain's farthest flung corners to experience the dramatic scenery and empty space. Not everyone is happy – some argue that the number of visitors is in danger of destroying what they come to find. However, the majority point out that the NC500 has breathed new life into the failing northern economy, generating revenue, taxes and jobs, and keeping shops, schools and petrol stations open.

Beyond argument is the fact that traffic on the NC500 is increasing annually, while the roads remain pretty much at their pre-2015 standard. In peak season, the single track roads are so busy that cars and camper-vans appear to be travelling in convoys, and accommodation can be at a premium. If you are able to be flexible with your dates, go in what the tourist professionals call 'the shoulder months' – either side of the peak season when traffic will be lighter and caravans fewer. Even the NC500 can be pretty dreary on a motorbike when you're following a nervous camper-van along an endless single track road. It's also easier to find somewhere to stay outside peak season. Consider doing the NC500 under canvas. Pre-booking accommodation can be restricting, while not pre-booking is very risky. On the other hand, places to pitch a tent in the wild are endless and the locations

are stunning. I prefer to do the circuit anti-clockwise, heading up the east coast to Wick. It's not taking anything away from the east coast by admitting that the west is top of the bill. On a practical note, with more distractions and excursions on the west it's easier to keep an eye on your schedule when you're nearing the end of the trip rather than close to the beginning.

Finally, try to leave time for side-tracks and detours. If you simply 'do the circuit', you'll probably fly past some delightful minor road that's waiting to be discovered. Overall, branding or no-branding, the NC500 roads are fabulous to ride, and the scenery is awe-inspiring. I've still got to visit the Cape Verde Islands, Tierra del Fuego and Huddersfield before I can confirm it but, yes, Condé Nast is probably right.

CEANNABEINNE, NEAR DURNESS

1 From Inverness take the A862 to Beauly (12 miles)

2 Continue on A862 through Dingwall to the north end of Cromarty Bridge (12 miles)

3 At the roundabout, go left onto A9 and follow signs to Wick (89 miles)

4 From Wick, continue north on the A99 to Reiss (3 miles)

5 At Reiss, turn right on A99 to John o' Groats (13 miles)

6 From John o' Groats harbour, return along A99 (0.5 miles)

7 Turn right onto A836 to Thurso, continuing through the town following signs for Scrabster (20 miles)

8 On leaving Thurso, rejoin A836 to Tongue (42 miles)

9 From Tongue, follow the A838 through Durness to Laxford Bridge (48 miles)

10 Continue ahead onto A894, signed Lochinver (18 miles)

11 Turn right onto B869 to Drumbeg and Lochinver (Coastal Route) (22 miles)

12 At T-junction, turn left onto A837 and follow signs to Ullapool (35 miles)

13 In Ullapool, head south on A836, signed Inverness (12 miles)

14 Turn right onto A832 to Gairloch (43 miles)

15 From Gairloch, continue on A832 to Kinlochewe (20 miles)

16 In Kinlochewe, turn right onto A896 to Shieldaig (18 miles)

17 From Shieldaig, continue on A896 to road junction (1 mile)

18 Turn right to Applecross (24 miles)

19 In Applecross, turn left for Lochcarron to T-junction (11 miles)

20 Turn right onto A896 to Lochcarron (6 miles)

21 From Lochcarron, continue on A896, then A890 to Achnasheen (20 miles)

22 Turn right onto A832 for Inverness (15 miles)

23 Turn right on A835 for Inverness to Contin (7 miles)

24 From Contin, continue on A835 to junction (2 miles)

25 Turn right onto A832 to Muir of Ord (5 miles)

26 In Muir of Ord, turn right onto A862 for Beauly and Inverness (15 miles)

HEADING SOUTH ON THE NC500

WHAT TO SEE

Dunrobin Castle (KW10 6SF); **Whaligoe Steps** (KW2 6AA); **Dunnet Head** (KW14 8XS); **Smoo Cave** (IV27 4PN); **Achmelvich Beach** (IV27 4JB); **Loch Maree** (IV22 2HL); the view from the top of the Bealach na Ba (IV54 8XF); **The Falls of Rogie** (IV14 9EQ)... the list is endless. The NC500 website is very helpful.

LOOK OUT FOR

There's a **zip-wire** operating on most days over the beach at Ceannabeinne (IV27 4QE), not far from Durness. Spectacular – just turn up and fly!

WHERE TO STAY

The **Bikers B&B** (IV7 8BB) at The Whitehouse, Conon Bridge, is billed as "Exclusive Accommodation for Motorcyclists". The guest book suggests it's not literally exclusive to bikers, but they really do like having bikers to stay. Decent rooms, comprehensive breakfast and well placed for the route.

The **Melvich Hotel** (KW14 7YJ) is a fine old roadside house with a couple of rather unsympathetic extensions, but inside it's warm and welcoming.

The Bothy in Tongue (IV27 4XG) is more modern, offering two rooms on the edge of the village. Stunning views and hospitality to match. Otherwise, the NC500 website has a full list of places to stay en route, but book well in advance.

WHERE TO EAT

There are countless places along the way. **Poppy's** in Golspie's Main Street (KW10 6RA) is handy on the east coast. **The Whale Tail** is hidden away on the Balnakeil Craft Village (IV27 4PT) in Durness but is well worth seeking out, and **The Whistle Stop Café** (IV22 2PF) at Kinlochewe is a good place to stop on the west coast. The NC500 website and app will help you find plenty of other places along the way.

Pentland Firth

Dunnet Head
Stroma

Dunnet Bay

Scrabster

Dunnet

Duncansby Head

John o' Groats

Strathy Point

Thurso

A99

A836

Strathy

Melvich

Keiss

Sinclair's Bay

Reay

Kyle of Tongue

Reiss

A838

Tongue

Bettyhill

A882

Wick

Noss Head

Caithness

Ben Loyal · 765

Loch Loyal

Thrumster

Altnabreac Station

Ulbster

Strath Naver

Syre

A99

Loch Naver

Forsinard

A897

Lybster

Altnaharra

Ben Klibreck · 982

Kinbrace

Morven 705

Latheron

Dunbeath

A836

Strath of Kildonan

Berriedale

Strath Brora

A9

Helmsdale

Lairg

Strath Fleet

A836

A839

2

Brora

Inversnaid

Golspie

Bonar Bridge

Evelix

Embo

Clashmore

Ardgay

A949

Dornoch

Dornoch Firth

Tarbat Ness

Struie 371

Tain

Portmahomack

r o s s

Kildary

Balintore

Loch Glass

A9

Alness

1

Invergordon

Nigg

Moray Firth

Lossiemouth

Evanton

Cromarty

A832

Buckie

A942

Dingwall

Black Isle

Rosemarkie

Nairn

Forres

A941

Elgin

A990

A98

A9

Fortrose

A96

Fochabers

A862

Tore

A940

A941

A95

Muir of Ord

Beauly

A96

A939

Craigellachie

A95

Keith

A833

INVERNESS

START

A920

Huntly

A82

Loch Ness

Grantown-on-Spey

A939

A95

A941

A97

A96

Drumnadrochit

A9

ROUTE 24
APPLECROSS AND LOCH EWE

TWISTY	■■■■	STRAIGHTER
SINGLE TRACK	■■■	WIDER

📍 **DISTANCE**
145 miles

🕐 **ALLOW**
4.5 hours

THE BEALACH NA BÀ

Ask 100 well-travelled bikers in Scotland to name the UK's most exhilarating road and the chances are that 90 of them would immediately say the Bealach na Bà.

The other ten might pause for a moment… and then probably name the same route. The road from Strathcarron to Applecross is the very definition of thrilling. Single track throughout, it climbs 2,000ft in just five miles, folding itself into the hillside, rocks to your right, safety barrier to your left, a wall of mountain ahead and a jaw-dropping view behind. A viewpoint at the top lets you catch your breath before the descent into Applecross. The Bealach na Bà (Gaelic for 'Pass of the Cattle') is a road you'll remember for the rest of your life. Why 'Pass of the Cattle'? In the 17th and 18th centuries, when cattle were central to the crofters' livelihoods, the livestock would be taken from Skye to Applecross and onward by 'drovers'. These hardy Highlanders assembled herds of cattle for the long walk to the sales in Crieff or Falkirk. The route we're taking was just a well-trodden track until 1822, and only given a tarmac surface in the 1950s – until then, the lifeline route into Applecross was by sea.

Today the Bealach na Bà is a mecca for cyclists, motorists and motorcyclists and, for a country road, it can be busy at the height of the season. On a motorbike, the joy of the Bealach can be tarnished if you find yourself following a campervan to the top, or having to pull in repeatedly to allow oncoming cars to pass. To get the best out of it, try to set off when the road is quiet – early morning or evening is best – and by staying locally the night before. It's certainly worth it because there is nothing quite like an uninterrupted run from bottom to the top. Beyond Applecross we head north on the 'Coast Road' – built in the 1970s – which undulates gently around the northern corner before it becomes a little more

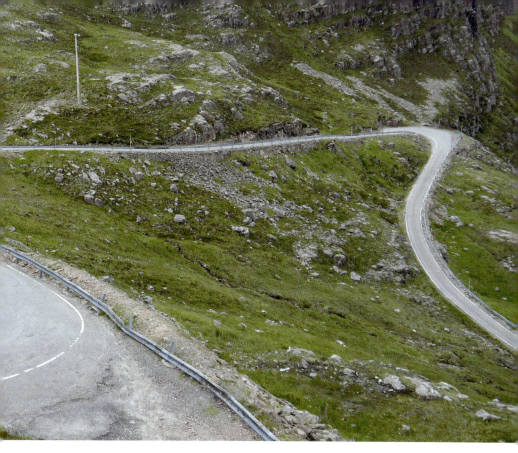

tight and technical from Kenmore to the head of Loch Shieldaig. Now we're off the leash on a good, wide road leading us past Shieldaig and up the side of Loch Maree to Gairloch and on to Poolewe, at the head of Loch Ewe. In the Second World War this was an important mustering point for Arctic convoys and, even today, there's a NATO refuelling station on the western shore. Two dead ends, one on either side of Loch Ewe, take us to an old anti-aircraft battery and the remains of the boom defence depot respectively.

Then we're back on the main road, passing Gruinard Island, where wartime chemical weapons experiments – with anthrax no less – made the island a no-go area for almost half a century. After

a fast run above Little Loch Broom we join the main road close by the National Nature Reserve at Corrieshalloch Gorge. From there, we can turn left for Ullapool, or go right (and right again after 19 miles) to return to Lochcarron.

LOCH CARRON

WHAT TO SEE

If the weather is good, stop at the **viewpoint on the summit of the Bealach na Bà** (IV54 8XF). On a clear day, the view over Skye to the Outer Hebrides is outstanding. At the viewpoint there is a useful 'topograph' to identify the different islands.

The **Anti Aircraft Battery** at Cove (IV22 2LT) was built to defend the convoys gathering in Loch Ewe to take vital supplies to Russia in the Second World War. Several gun emplacements and searchlight buildings remain, along with many concrete bases of accommodation huts. It's also the site of a tragic shipwreck when 60 crew members of a US liberty ship were lost when it went aground in a storm in 1944. Local crofters performed heroics to rescue the 14 survivors.

Turn right at Kinlochewe (before No.5) and head along the A832 for three miles to the **Glen Docherty Viewpoint**. The view is the cover shot for this book.

LOOK OUT FOR

The **massive dry dock at Kishorn** (IV54 8XA). It was built to construct North Sea oil platforms in the 1970s when two old cruise ships were brought in to accommodate the

3,000-strong workforce. After being used to fabricate the supports for the Skye Bridge, the dock was idle for over 20 years. In 2017, it was announced that it would be recommissioned to help construct installations for the Kincardine Offshore Windfarm Project.

WHERE TO STAY

There are several good B&Bs in Lochcarron. We recommend the **Sithean** (IV54 8YH) – pronounced 'She'un' – or the Loch Dubh (IV54 8YA), pronounced 'Loch Doo'. The **Kinlochewe Hotel** (IV22 2PA) has a bunkhouse which is basic but clean and cheap.

WHERE TO EAT

The **Waterside Café** (IV54 8YD) in Lochcarron is superb, while the **Applecross Inn** (IV54 8LR) is popular – for good reason – but often pretty busy. Try the **Potting Shed Café** (IV54 8ND) in the gardens at Applecross House. They grow their own veg and catch their own fish. Locally sourced? You bet.

Coast Coffee Company (IV21 2BQ) is down by the pier in Gairloch. Great coffee and a good-looking menu. Closed in winter. Or the **Bridge Cottage Café** (IV22 2JU) in Poolewe, which is open all year round.

1 In Lochcarron, with the water to your left, take A896 towards Shieldaig (7 miles)

2 Turn left, signed Applecross (11 miles)

3 Turn right at T-junction in Applecross, signed Shieldaig (24 miles)

4 Turn left at T-junction onto A896 to Kinlochewe (18 miles)

5 Turn left onto A832 to Gairloch and continue to Poolewe (25 miles)

6 Turn left onto B8057, through Inverasdale, to car park at the far end (9 miles)

7 Return to Poolewe (9 miles)

8 Turn left onto A832 to Aultbea (6 miles)

9 Turn left, to Mellon Charles (3 miles)

10 Return to Altbea (3 miles)

11 Turn left onto A832 to T-junction (32 miles)

12 For Ullapool, turn left (12 miles) or to return to Lochcarron, turn right and right again in 19 miles, then follow signs (60 miles)

APPLECROSS

THE BLACK ISLE AND STRATH BRORA

TWISTY	STRAIGHTER
SINGLE TRACK	WIDER

DISTANCE
145 miles

ALLOW
4 hours

Spoiler alert! The Black Isle is not an island. And it's not black.

It's mostly green and it's just a peninsula pretending to be an island. The Black Isle does have a ferry service, operating across the Cromarty Firth in the summer months, but it's quite easy to drive round by road if the boat's not running. So the name is a bit misleading, but don't let that put you off going there. Once you turn off the A9 north of Inverness, the Black Isle certainly has an island feel about it; it's surrounded by water on three sides with little coastal communities clustered around their harbours. The fishing fleets have long since gone, with the harbours now populated mostly by pleasure craft.

From Avoch to Fortrose the road runs close to the shore before climbing from Rosemarkie to follow the shoulder of the hillside overlooking the Moray Firth. Along the way, we detour out to Chanonry Point, which reaches over a mile into the sea; a peninsula on a peninsula, jutting out towards the post-Jacobite garrison of Fort George on the other side. Then we're up on the Eathie road making for Cromarty, riding high along the Black Isle's shoulder with views across to Fort George. Cromarty

THE CROMARTY FIRTH

is an attractive wee corner, well worth exploring as you wait for the ferry to take you across the narrows to Nigg. If the ferry isn't running it's a 36-mile trip round the Cromarty Firth to get to the other side – just keep the water to your right hand (it'll be on both sides as you cross the Cromarty Bridge, obviously) until you rejoin this route by Tain. It gives you the chance to get a good look at the oil rig graveyard in the Cromarty Firth – the rigs are waiting for the industry to pick up or for the scrap man to come calling. The tiny ferry carries us across the mouth of the firth, between the craggy headlands – called The Sutors of Cromarty – to a slipway by the Nigg fabrication yard, now rebranded as an Energy Park.

Then we're passing Tain to take the old road round the Dornoch Firth, via Bonar Bridge, before heading into Dornoch itself. This charming but busy backwater was where Madonna and Guy Ritchie got married in 2000. We pass the turning to Embo – a village that famously declared itself independent for a day in 1988 to raise funds to buy the local school – and follow the shore of Loch Fleet back to the A9. We pass through Golspie to Brora, where we leave the beaten track onto a narrow road leading into Strath Brora. Loch Brora is a gem; peaceful, picturesque, unspoiled and comparatively unknown, it even has wee sandy beaches for our enjoyment. The road leads in a wide arc before dropping down into Strath Fleet to join the wider, faster highway at

Pittentrail. We can pick the pace up as we head for Lairg, then Bonar Bridge, before cutting over the brilliant Struie Road to Evanton. From there we can either join the A9 over the Cromarty Bridge, or divert through Dingwall, following signs to Inverness to lead back to the Tore roundabout.

SOUNDTRACK

Taste the Coast
by Admiral Fallow

FURTHER READING

Amnesia by Michael Ridpath (Corvus, 2017). A 'did-he-do-it?' novel set near the Black Isle's western boundary.

1 From Tore roundabout (IV6 7RZ), five miles north of Inverness on the A9, turn east onto A832 to Fortrose (9 miles)

2 At the far end of the High Street, turn right onto Ness Road to Chanonry Point (1.5 miles)

3 Return along Ness Road until you can turn right to the Golf Club (almost 1 mile)

4 Follow the road beside the sea until it turns inland to the Plough Inn at Rosemarkie (1 mile)

5 Turn right, unsigned, onto A832 (1 mile)

6 Turn right to Eathie and follow the road to T-junction (7 miles)

7 Turn right into A832 to Cromarty (1.5 miles)

8 Take the ferry **Note:** Alternatively, follow the B9163 to the Cromarty Bridge, the A9 to Tain (36 miles)

9 After disembarking the ferry, take first exit at the roundabout and follow the B9175 to the A9 (7 miles)

10 Take 2nd exit on roundabout, signed Tain, and follow signs to Bonar Bridge (19 miles)

11 In Bonar Bridge, follow road, now A949, round to right to T-junction with A9 (10 miles)

12 Turn left on A9 (1.3 miles)

13 Refuelling opportunity is a few hundred yards up the A9 to your right

14 Turn right to rejoin A949 to Dornoch (2 miles)

15 At the end of the High Street, turn left onto Station Road

16 Follow the road, which narrows as you pass the sign to Embo, to T-junction with A9 (6 miles)

17 Turn right onto A9 to Brora (11 miles)

18 Immediately after crossing the river, turn left, signed Gordonbush, and follow the road to Pittentrail (17 miles)

19 Turn right onto A839 to Lairg (10 miles)

20 Turn left onto A836 to Bonar Bridge (10 miles)

21 Turn right on A836, signed Tain, to road junction (4 miles)

22 Turn right onto B9176, signed Dingwall (15 miles)

23 Turn right on the A9 back to Tore roundabout (12 miles)

WHAT TO SEE

Bottlenose dolphins. Chanonry Point (IV10 8SD) is probably the best place in Britain to stand on land and watch dolphins in the sea. When the tide is rising, they can often be seen hunting and playing in the turbulent waters just off the point.

LOOK OUT FOR

The Clootie Well (IV8 8PB) by the roadside as you head for Munlochy. This ancient spring is alleged to heal the sick, provided they leave a cloot (cloth) tied to a tree nearby. As the cloth degrades, so the illness eases. It probably worked better before synthetic materials – now it's more like an explosion at a jumble sale.

WHERE TO STAY

Fearn Hotel (IV20 1TJ) is a few miles north of the ferry, just off the road to Tain. Accommodation includes three single ensuite rooms. Clean, friendly and good value.

Sleeperzzz (IV28 3XA) is a hostel in old railway carriages beside the station at Rogart, with mostly bunk beds in sleeper-carriages, and a showman's caravan. Or there's a one room B&B in the waiting room, but the breakfast falls short of 'hearty'.

WHERE TO EAT

Fortrose Café (IV10 8SU) on the High Street is busy with locals – always a good sign! Cosy and a great choice of food.

Linda's (KW9 6NY) in Brora does straightforward fayre, but does it very well. And for a very reasonable price.

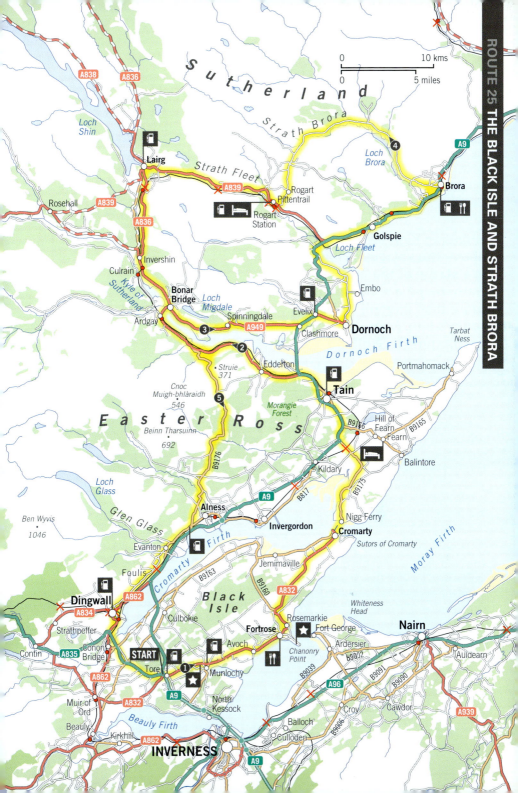

TAIN TO TONGUE

TWISTY — STRAIGHTER	**DISTANCE** 166 miles
SINGLE TRACK — WIDER	**ALLOW** 4.5 hours

Standing high on a hilltop above the village of Golspie is a statue of the first Duke of Sutherland, a man who did more than anyone to create today's empty landscape in northernmost Scotland.

The Duke ordered the eviction of countless families to clear the land for sheep. The 'Highland Clearances' were a form of ethnic cleansing – the richest in the land (and the Duke of Sutherland was exactly that) burning the poorest out of their homes. Some 15,000 people were driven off the Duke's estates between 1811 and 1821. This circuit leads through the land he cleared and passes the statue raised in his memory (although there are occasional campaigns to have it taken down).

The road dazzles from the outset as we ignore the Dornoch Bridge and head along the southern side of the Dornoch Firth – before the bridge all traffic for the far north had to pass this way – to Bonar Bridge and up to Lairg. Then it's single track with passing places as we follow the river up onto the high ground. There's nothing but moorland, heather and forestry for company on the climb to the splendidly isolated Crask Inn, before dropping into Strath Vagastie to

THE KYLE OF TONGUE AND BEN LOYAL

Altnaharra. You haven't passed a turn-off in 20 miles and you won't see another for 15 until you reach Tongue, passing Loch Naver and Loch Loyal on the way. (If you've never been to Scotland's north coast before, it's worth making a 20-minute detour left from Tongue to enjoy the view over Loch Eriboll.)

After taking a turn round the Kyle of Tongue, we head east, picking up the pace as we make for Bettyhill where the Duchess of Sutherland built a village for displaced crofters. Magnanimously, she named it after herself. We head back inland from Bettyhill on single track

surface, which follows the meandering River Naver up to the loch of the same name. It's all peace and tranquility now, but Strathnaver was the scene of some of the most notorious clearances to take place anywhere in Scotland. Just over a mile from Syre, the Duke's henchman torched a house with 92-year-old Margaret Mackay still inside. The court found him not guilty of arson or culpable homicide. From Syre, we cross over the moorland to Strathbeg and into the Strath of Kildonan, where evictions caused the population to drop from 1,500 to 250 in 20 years. It's a captivating trip downriver to Helmsdale, where we join the A9 for a canter down the coast to Brora, Golspie – note the statue on the hill – and on to Tain.

SOUNDTRACK

Slow French Waltz by Nick Keir. For no other reason than it's a fine song by one of Scotland's many fine songwriters.

FURTHER READING

Writing on the Road: Campervan Love and the Joy of Solitude by Sue Reid Sexton (Waverley, 2016). We see enough of them on the road – this gives us a chance to understand the mindset.

THE NC500, SUTHERLAND

1 From Tain, take the A9, signed Thurso, to roundabout before Dornoch Bridge (2 miles)

2 Take the first exit onto A836 to Bonar Bridge (13 miles)

3 After crossing the bridge, turn left on A836 to Lairg and follow it to T-junction by Tongue (48 miles)

4 Turn left onto A838, through Tongue and over the causeway (3 miles)

5 Turn left, signed Kinloch, to ride round the Kyle of Tongue and back to the village (9 miles)

6 Turn right, onto A836, signed Thurso, to Bettyhill (13 miles)

7 Return from Bettyhill to road junction (3 miles)

8 Turn left onto B871 to Syre (9 miles)

9 Just before a white kirk with a red roof, turn left onto B871 and follow signs to Helmsdale (34 miles)

10 In Helmsdale, go left on the roundabout (250 yards)

11 Turn right onto A9 back to Tain (33 miles)

WHAT TO SEE

From Altnaharra, take a detour on the B873 along Loch Naver to the remains of the crofting township of **Grummore** (IV27 4UE). It sits in the grass and heather just up the hillside from the caravan site. In 1819, 16 houses were set alight to drive out the occupants.

The Emigrants Statue (KW8 6JZ), on the left as you leave Helmsdale, was originally planned as a 30ft monument for the top of the hill overlooking the village. It was intended to rival the statue of the Duke overlooking Golspie further south (KW10 6UE).

LOOK OUT FOR

Salmon leaping the River Helmsdale. Maybe I was just lucky as I rode by (in July) but I nearly fell off in surprise.

WHERE TO STAY

For a spot of roadside remoteness, you can't better **The Crask Inn** (IV27 4AB). Now owned by the Scottish Episcopal Church and in the middle of nowhere (between Lairg and Altnahara), it welcomes travellers regardless of their religious beliefs. The room rate is very reasonable to start with, but as it includes an evening meal and breakfast, frankly, it's a bargain!

WHERE TO EAT

La Mirage (KW8 6JA) in Helmsdale is well known for the quality of its fish suppers… less so for the accuracy of its French grammar.

Weavers Café (IV27 4XW) just east of Tongue is very good but, like lots of the eateries in this area, it can get busy!

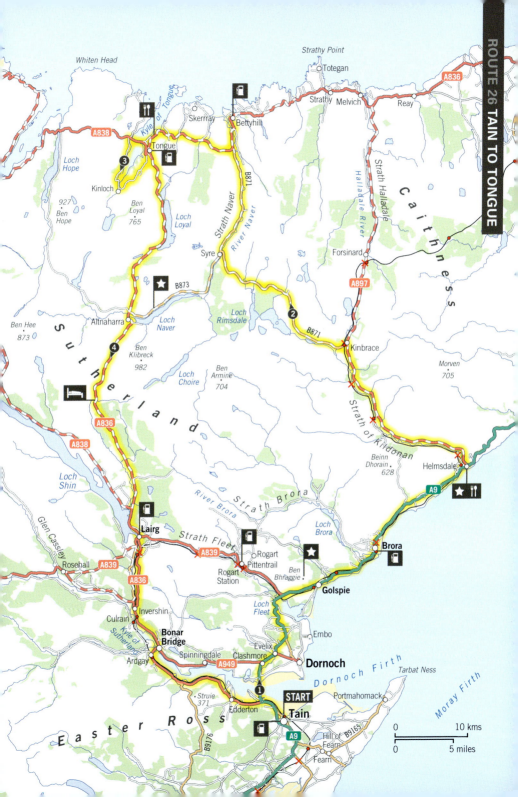

A836

Whiten Head

Strathy Point

Totegan

Strathy

Melvich

Reay

Kyle of Tongue

Skerray

Bettyhill

Tongue

A838

Loch
Hope

Strath Halladale

Halladale River

C a i t h n e s s

Kinloch

3

Ben
Loyal
765

Ben
Hope
927

Loch
Loyal

B871

Strath Naver

River Naver

Syre

Loch
Rimsdale

2

B871

Forsinard

A897

Kinbrace

Ben Hee
873

Altnaharra

B873

Loch
Naver

Loch
Choire

Ben
Klibreck
982

Ben
Armine
704

Morven
705

4

S u t h e r l a n d

A836

Strath of Kildonan

Beinn
Dhorain
628

Helmsdale

A9

A838

Loch
Shin

River Brora

Strath Brora

Loch
Brora

Brora

Glen Cassley

Lairg

Strath Fleet

A839

Rogart

Pittentrail

Rogart
Station

Ben
Bhraggie

Golspie

Rosehall

A839

A836

Invershin

Culrain

Kyle of
Sutherland

Bonar
Bridge

Spinningdale

A949

Ardgay

Evelix

Clashmore

Loch
Fleet

Embo

Dornoch

Dornoch Firth

Tarbat Ness

1

**START
Tain**

Struie
371

Edderton

Portmahomack

Moray Firth

A9

Hill of
Fearn

B9165

Fearn

E a s t e r   R o s s

B9176

| 0 | | 10 kms |
| 0 | | 5 miles |

SKIBO TO SCOURIE

LOCH ASSYNT

TWISTY	STRAIGHTER	**DISTANCE** 137 miles
SINGLE TRACK	WIDER	**ALLOW** 3hrs 15m

As you power out over the moors that separate Scotland's east and west coasts, it's sobering to reflect that more than half the land in Scotland is still owned by fewer than 500 people.

Think of vast, sprawling sporting estates that ring to the sound of gunfire; grouse and pheasants falling like autumn leaves; ponies carrying dead deer from the hills; tweed jackets; Range Rovers; and the smell of waxed jacket and wet spaniel. In recent years, many Highland estates have changed hands, with titled owners flogging off the family silver to rich investors from overseas who are keen to wear tweed and shoot things. So when a bunch of crofters in Assynt succeeded in buying the 21,000-acre North Lochinver Estate in 1993, a collective cheer went up from the naturally left-leaning Scottish population. The crofters had waged a canny campaign, and found moral and financial support pouring in from across the nation. Twelve years later, the local community purchased a further 44,000 acres from the Vesteys, one of Britain's richest families and among Scotland's largest landowners. The Assynt crofters inspired dozens of other communities to take control of local land, from small-scale village plots to entire islands like Gigha and Eigg.

So it's fitting that this route begins by crossing the Dornoch Firth close to Skibo Castle, an exclusive private club for the rich and famous, and leads to the humble crofts of Assynt on the opposite coast. From the Dornoch Bridge, we head up the A9 a short while before turning into Strath Fleet. The railway keeps us company up the gentle valley and onto the moor – a good road to Lairg. Then we join the A838, mostly a single track road, following Loch Shin and a series of smaller lochs to Laxford Bridge. The carriageway may be narrow, but the surface is fine and the sight lines are good, making for quick progress through the hills.

On turning south, we share the road with the NC500, so it will be busier, looping through Scourie and Badcall to the bridge at Kylesku. It's worth stopping to admire what must surely be one of the most beautiful concrete crossings ever built, curving across the narrow stretch of water. Many modern bridges spoil the surroundings, but in Kylesku the bridge enhances the wild Sutherland landscape around it. Before it was opened in 1984, travellers used a ferry to cross the narrows. If the ferry couldn't run, it required a 100-mile detour via Lairg! The water to the west is Loch Cairnbawn, which served as the training base for the X-craft, the midget submarines that crippled the German battleship *Tirpitz* in a Norwegian fjord in 1943. Then we're climbing again between the mountains until we can

drop down to Loch Assynt, passing Ardvreck Castle on our way to the road junction at Ledmore. Here the NC500 turns right, while we continue on a single track road – but one that allows for a fast run home – along the River Oykel and the Kyles of Sutherland, back to Bonar Bridge and the Dornoch Firth.

SOUNDTRACK

Far Side Of The World by Tide Lines

FURTHER READING

The Poor Had No Lawyers: Who Owns Scotland (and How They Got it) by Andy Wightman (Birlinn, 2015)

FANAGMORE

1 From Dornoch Bridge roundabout (IV19 1JX) go north on the A9, signed Thurso (11 miles)

2 After crossing the bridge over Loch Fleet, turn left onto A839 to T-junction in Lairg (15 miles) **Note:** It would be sensible to refuel in Lairg before continuing!

3 Turn right onto A836, signed Tongue (3 miles)

4 Turn left onto A838 to T-junction (35 miles)

5 Turn left onto A894, signed Scourie, continuing to T-junction at Loch Assynt (23 miles)

6 Turn left onto A837, signed Ullapool (8 miles)

7 When the main road to Ullapool road turns sharp right, continue ahead on A837, and follow signs to Bonar Bridge (30 miles)

8 Turn right on A836, signed Tain, to return to the Dornoch Bridge (12 miles)

WHAT TO SEE

The ruins by Loch Assynt. These include **Ardvreck Castle**, a MacLeod stronghold until it was seized by the MacKenzies in 1672. After half a century, Mrs MacKenzie persuaded her man to build a fancy classical gaff along the road. He obliged, but the construction of Calda House bankrupted him. The family torched the place to make sure no other clan could move in.

LOOK OUT FOR

The **Maid of Kylesku** ferry boat. Turn left after crossing the Kylesku bridge and stop in the car park. Across the other side of the water you can see the old ferry that carried four cars at a time across the loch before the bridge was built. The Maid of Kylesku was simply driven ashore and abandoned in 1967 when she was no longer required.

A minor road which turns off to the right about 3.5 miles after Laxford Bridge. It's signposted to Tarbet and Fanagmore (IV27 4SU) and offers a lovely little lollipop-shaped detour, adding about eight miles to your journey.

WHERE TO STAY

The **Inchnadamph Hotel** (IV27 4HN) is an old coaching inn providing decent accommodation in a lovely location and at a sensible price. Closed in the winter.

WHERE TO EAT

The Anchorage (IV27 4TG) in Scourie does good food for the road. It's right by the road as well. **The Pier Café/Restaurant** (IV27 4EG) in Lairg. Unpretentious and inexpensive.

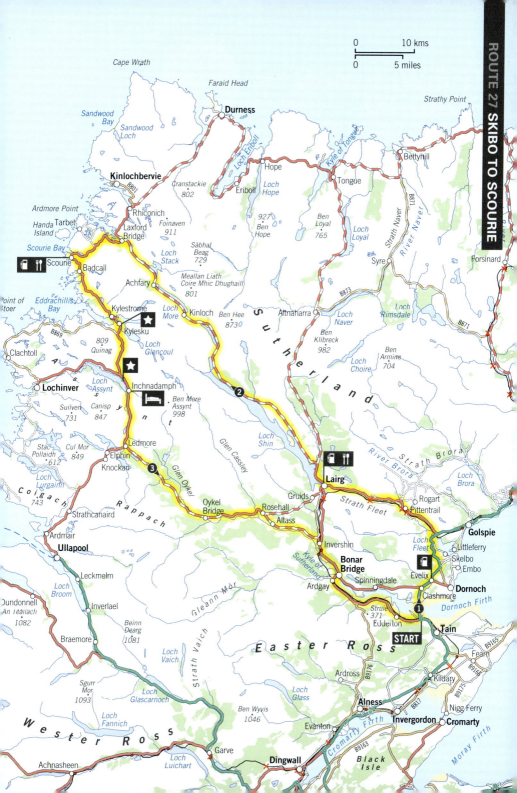

ROUTE 28
THE WEE MAD ROAD TO ACHILTIBUIE

TWISTY	STRAIGHTER
SINGLE TRACK	WIDER

DISTANCE
100 miles

ALLOW
3.5 hours

THE SUMMER ISLES

In a country where people like to give descriptive names to roads – think Rest and Be Thankful, Pass of the Cattle and Tak-Ma-Doon – nothing quite sums up a stretch of tarmac so succinctly as The Wee Mad Road in Sutherland.

Strictly speaking, the Wee Mad Road is south of Lochinver, but the name could equally well apply to the B869 to the north, which convolutes its way around the coastline of Assynt through Stoer and Drumbeg. In a part of the world where no road is ordinary, these roads are truly extraordinary, and utterly enthralling.

As we set off uphill from Ullapool we're quickly into a different kind of landscape, where the mountains form islands in the heather, almost like lumps in a carpet. There's a term for them, apparently – 'inselbergs', or island mountains. It's a splendid road that takes us north, over to rejoin the sea at Ardmair before turning inland, the tarmac fast and flowing all the way. Ignore the sign to Achiltibuie (that's for our return) and enjoy the sweeping corners and long straights to Loch Assynt. Tempting as it is to continue

along the water's edge, we turn off to maintain a northerly heading for another few miles to the Drumbeg road. (At this point we're a couple of miles short of Kylesku, so if you've yet to see the bridge there, you might want to carry on before coming back to join the Drumbeg road.)

The fun continues as we set off to Drumbeg on the single track surface with sudden steep hills, blind summits and disappearing corners. You'll be working your way up and down the gears like a piper practising his scales, but the experience will gladden your heart. Once through Stoer and Clachtoll, we're dodging between rocky hillocks until we come over the summit, with one of Scotland's most iconic mountains – Suilven – in the distance. Lochinver is a laid back fishing village and a good place to refuel and refresh before the 'wee madness' to come. At times

you'll feel like you're riding along the beach, at others it's like sidestepping your way through a crowd, and at one point there's only a low, stone wall keeping you from dropping into the sea. You need to concentrate but, if you don't hurry, there's time to enjoy the scenery along the way. The Wee Mad Road ends at Loch Bad a' Ghaill, but the single track continues as we head further into the remote Coigach wilderness and pass Achnahaird Beach on our way to Achiltibuie, the best known of several scattered communities along the peninsula.

There are probably many reasons to visit Achiltibuie, but first among them must be the setting (last among them will be the architecture!) – it's a magical view out across the bay to the Summer Isles and the mountains beyond. Grab a coffee from the Piping School, put your feet up and think about the meaning of life. When you're ready, get back on the bike for the return to Ullapool, skirting the base of another of Scotland's most famous mountains, Stac Pollaidh, and rejoining the main road at the junction we passed earlier.

SOUNDTRACK

New Dawn by The Mad Ferret Band. You might not have heard it before but you'll be singing along by the second verse.

FURTHER READING

At the Loch of the Green Corrie by Andrew Greig (Quercus, 2010). Shortly before he died, the poet Norman McCaig told the author to go and catch a fish in an unidentified loch in Assynt, McCaig's favourite part of Scotland. This is part memoir, part homage to the great man.

↑ **1** With the petrol station on the seafront to your right, set off along the road towards Ullapool harbour (100 yards)

↱ **2** Turn right on the A835, signed Kylesku, to Inchnadamph (23 miles)

↑ **3** Continue along the side of Loch Assynt, past Ardvreck Castle ruins, to road junction (2 miles)

⊢ **4** Turn right onto A894, signed Kylesku, to road junction (5 miles)

⊣ **5** Turn left onto B869, through Drumbeg and Stoer, to T-junction (22 miles)

⊤ **6** Turn right onto A837 to Lochinver (0.5 miles)

↑ **7** Continue through Lochinver (with water to your right) to pedestrian crossing with lights

⊣ **8** Turn left, signed Achiltibuie, and follow the road to T-junction (12 miles)

⊤ **9** Turn right to the next T-junction, beside an information board (3 miles)

⊤ **10** Turn right (both directions go to Achiltibuie, left is shorter) (8 miles)

↓ **11** Turn round! From Achiltibuie, with the sea to your left, follow the road back to a right-hand junction, by the information board passed earlier (2.5 miles)

⊢ **12** Turn right and follow signs back to Ullapool (21 miles)

THE WEE MAD ROAD

WHAT TO SEE

The Summer Isle close up. **Boat trips** around the isles run three times a day from the harbour at Old Dornie (IV26 2YP), just north of Achiltibuie. Book in advance at www.summerisles-seatours.co.uk

LOOK OUT FOR

Distracted motorists! Twisty roads and a scenic backdrop mean you need to keep your wits about you.

WHERE TO STAY

Croft 338 (IV27 4NW) in Drumbeg. Good accommodation with a brilliant breakfast. For an evening meal, the Drumbeg Hotel is a five-minute walk along the road.

The **Riverside Guest House** (IV26 2UE) in Ullapool is a first-rate B&B on the edge of town.

WHERE TO EAT

Flossie's at the Clachtoll campsite (IV27 4JD). It's a photo-opp as well as a good place to eat.

Lochinver Larder (IV27 4JY). It's a pie shop, a coffee shop and a bistro rolled into one. The pies are famous and freshly baked. Buy a savoury pie for the main and a fruit one for dessert.

Am Fuaran (IV26 2YR) is a cosy wee bar in Altandhu, just north of Achiltibuie. Good food and a lovely view!

The **Achiltibuie Piping School Café** (IV26 2YF) is a welcome stop at the end of a long road. And there's a wonderful view out to the Summer Isles.

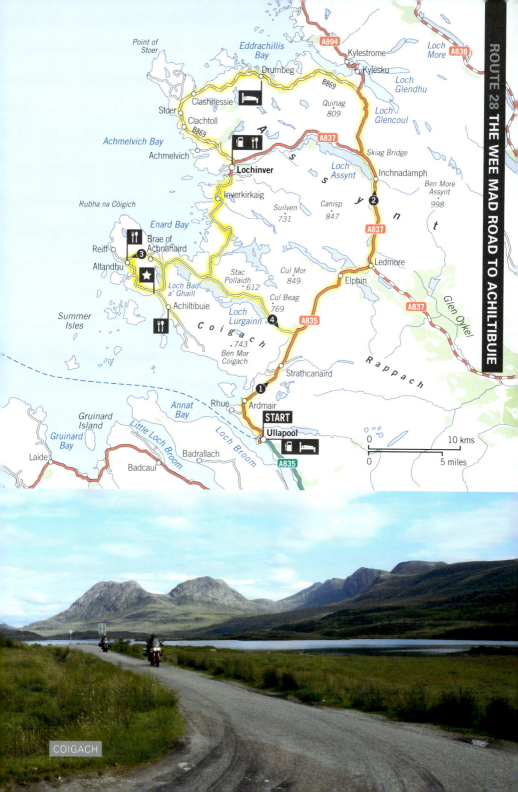

Point of
Stoer

Eddrachillis
Bay

A894

Kylestrome

Kylesku

Loch
More

A838

Drumbeg

B869

Loch
Glendhu

Clashnessie

Quinag
809

Loch
Glencoul

Stoer

Clachtoll

B869

A837

Skiag Bridge

Inchnadamph

Ben More
Assynt
998

Achmelvich Bay

Achmelvich

Lochinver

Loch
Assynt

A
s
s
y
n
t

2

Inverkirkaig

Suilven
731

Canisp
847

A837

Rubha na Còigich

Enard Bay

Reiff

Brae of
Achnahaird

3

Ledmore

A837

Altandhu

Loch Bad
a' Ghaill

Cul Mor
849

Stac
Pollaidh
612

Elphin

Glen Oykel

Achiltibuie

Cul Beag
769

Summer
Isles

Loch
Lurgainn

4

A835

C o i g a c h

.743

Ben Mor
Coigach

R a p p a c h

Strathcanaird

Annat
Bay

Rhue

Ardmair

1

Gruinard
Island

START

Ullapool

Gruinard
Bay

Little Loch Broom

Loch Broom

Laide

Badrallach

0   10 kms

A835

Badcaul

0   5 miles

COIGACH

TWISTY	STRAIGHTER	**DISTANCE** 90 miles
SINGLE TRACK	WIDER	**ALLOW** Stay 2 nights

NO STOPPING ON CAUSEWAY

DRIVERS CROSS AT OWN RISK

THE CHURCHILL BARRIERS

Most people who come this far north will knock off a few pictures at John o' Groats without even considering the logical next step – a short ferry trip across the Pentland Firth to Orkney.

Those who make the crossing – from either Gills Bay or Stromness – will find it amply repays the ferry fare, with great roads and wonderful scenery. Orkney (never call the islands 'the Orkneys') is quite unlike the rest of Scotland – Orkney and Shetland are proud of their Scandinavian roots and the islands still have a strong Norse flavour. To make the most of the Orkney roads, travel with Pentland Ferries from Gills Bay to St Margaret's Hope. From there it's a brilliant run to Kirkwall, skipping along a chain of islands across the Churchill Barriers built by Italian prisoners of war, as we skirt the wartime anchorage of Scapa Flow. Then it's onto the Holm Straight, where local bikers go to see what their machines are capable of. The road leads into the islands' capital, Kirkwall, with the ancient and impressive St Magnus Cathedral at its heart.

Next it's west to Finstown, named after a man called Finn who opened a pub there in 1811. He left after four years but the village has kept his name ever since. Another long straight carries us

north before we round the top of the Westmainland, with fine views out over the Rousay, and outer isles. We pass the Brough of Birsay, connected by a tidal causeway to the mainland, and the ruins of the Bishop's Palace as we turn to head south. A highlight – although a busy one – is the village of Skara Brae, which was buried by sand in prehistoric times only to re-emerge after a storm in 1850 complete with undisturbed stone furniture and fittings! Then we make for the old port at Stromness, where once ships docked before sailing for Hudson's Bay in Canada. Now it's the base for divers exploring the First World War German battleships that were sunk

in Scapa Flow. Stromness can probably claim the narrowest main street in Britain and vehicles can use it in both directions! Our route back east includes extraordinary emerging archaeology, along with famous standing stones, at Brodgar and the prehistoric tomb at Maeshowe – 'The Heart of Neolithic Orkney'. Then we head up to one of the highest points on the Orkney mainland where the islands are spread out below you like a blanket. That's on a good day; on a poor one, miss that bit out! Orkney is not hard to reach from Caithness – you won't regret making the crossing, but don't try to do it all in a day!

SOUNDTRACK

The Folky Gibbon by The Chair – a spirited band with an oddly recumbent name.

FURTHER READING

Cox's Navy: Salvaging the German High Seas Fleet at Scapa Flow 1924–1931 by Tony Booth (Pen & Sword, 2011). How a scrap merchant with no experience led the operation to salvage the German High Seas Fleet that had been scuttled in Scapa Flow in 1919.

🚢 **1** Catch the ferry from Gills Bay (KW1 4YB) to St Margaret's Hope

↰ **2** Turn left from the ferry and follow signs for Kirkwall (15 miles)

↑ **3** From Kirkwall, with the water to your right, take the A965 signed Stromness, to Finstown (7 miles)

↦ **4** Turn right onto A966, signposted to Tingwall Jetty and Evie Village, to Birsay (17 miles)

↰ **5** Turn left (or right if you have visited the ruined palace or Brough of Birsay) onto A967, signed Dounby (1 mile)

↦ **6** Turn right by the old school, now a hostel, onto B9056 to crossroads at Quoyloo (4 miles)

↦ **7** Turn right, still on B9056, past Bay of Skaill to follow signs to Stromness (9 miles)

↑ **8** From Stromness, put the water on your right and follow Ferry Road to a roundabout (500 yards)

↱ **9** Turn right onto Cairston Road to junction with A965 (2 miles)

↱ **10** Turn right (no signs) onto A965, through Stenness to left hand junction (2 miles)

↰ **11** Turn left onto B9055 to visit Standing Stones and Ring of Brodgar (1.4 miles)

↓ **12** Return to A965 and turn right, to Stenness (1.5 miles)

↰ **13** Turn left opposite the filling station, soon bending right to pass the school and continue over the hill to T-junction (1.5 miles)

↰ **14** Turn left onto A964, passing the Houton ferry terminal, through Orphir to Marness Garage (10 miles)

↰ **15** Half a mile beyond the garage, turn left onto unclassified road, signed Broomfield (1.5 miles)

↰ **16** Turn left for 200 yards, then turn right and follow the road to the top of Wideford Hill (1 mile)

↓ **17** Return down the hill and turn left to T-junction (2 miles)

↰ **18** Turn left into Wellington Street to T-junction (200 yards)

↰ **19** Turn left to go into town, or right to return to the ferry (15 miles)

WHAT TO SEE

You can't miss the **Churchill Barriers** that carry the road from island to island, but watch out for the tiny **Italian Chapel** (KW17 2RT) on the right before you cross your fourth barrier – it was built by Italian prisoners in the Second World War. The ancient village of **Skara Brae** (KW16 3LR) provides a snapshot of life from 5,000 years ago, while the (unstaffed) **Orkneyinga Saga Centre** in Orphir (KW17 2RD) gives a good insight into the island's Viking past. It's worth getting a ferry from Houton (KW17 2RD) to the **Scapa Flow Visitor Centre and Museum** at Lyness on Hoy. It shines a fascinating spotlight on Orkney's pivotal role in the two World Wars. If you take your bike on the ferry make sure you book in advance with Orkney Ferries.

LOOK OUT FOR

Sunken ships beside the causeways between St Margaret's Hope and Kirkwall. When Scapa Flow was a major naval base in the First World War, redundant ships were sunk between the islands to block the channels. **Roadsigns pointing to Twatt**. A photo opportunity?

WHERE TO STAY

The Peedie Hostel (KW15 1QX) provides good budget accommodation in Kirkwall. **The West End Hotel** (KW15 1BU) – it's reasonably priced, does good food and has private parking round the back. Don't let the fact that this is a former 'isolation' hospital put you off! There's a great campsite at **Wheems Organic Farm** in South Ronaldsay (KW17 2TJ), with camping pods if you prefer.

WHERE TO EAT

Try **Archive Coffee** (KW15 1NW) in Kirkwall's Laing Street, part of the Old Library complex. Or **Julia's Café** (KW16 3AE), opposite the ferry terminal in Stromness.

Westray

*Westray
Firth*

Faray

*Sacquoy
Head*

Scock
Ness

Eday

Rousay

Westness

Egilsay

*Costa
Head*

3

Broch of Birsay

Birsay

Twatt

A967

Evie

Tingwall

Wyre

Marwick
Head

*Mid Tooin
221*

A966

Skara Brae

Quoyloo

Dounby

Gorseness

Shapinsay

A965

Balfour

Yesnaby

Voy

*Wide
Firth*

Rerwick
Head

Mull
Head

A967

*Ring of
Brodgar*

Finstown

2

A965

KIRKWALL

Breck Ness

Stenness

*Wideford
Hill*

*Ward Hill
• 269*

*Keelylang
Hill*

Stromness

Kirbister

Orphir

4

A964

Tankerness

A961

A960

Moaness

*Ward Hill
• 481*

Houton

*Old Man
of Hoy*

*Knap of
Trowieglen
399*

*Scapa
Flow*

St Mary's

Rose Ness

*Rora
Head*

Rackwick

Hoy

Flotta

Burray

Lyness

St. Margaret's Hope

1

START

Longhope

*South
Ronaldsay*

Widewall

A961

Brims

South Walls

Swona

Burwick

Pentland   Firth

*Brough
Ness*

Stroma

Dunnet Head

Stroma

B855

Gills

*Duncansby
Head*

Mey

John o' Groats

*Dunnet
Bay*

Dunnet

Scrabster

Castletown

A99

Thurso

0		10 kms
0		5 miles

SHETLAND

ST NINIAN'S ISLE

TWISTY · STRAIGHTER	**DISTANCE** 215 miles
SINGLE TRACK · WIDER	**ALLOW** 4 days

If you fancy a foreign holiday but can't find your passport, consider Shetland.

It's as foreign as you can get without currency conversion, and it's quite an adventure to get there. A twelve-hour ferry journey from Aberdeen (or a mere eight hours from Orkney) puts you ashore in Lerwick and from the moment you step ashore, it's just like being abroad; different landscape, different architecture, different accent, different place names. Shetland doesn't feel like Scotland and Shetlanders don't really think of themselves as Scottish. You can hear the Scandinavian heritage in the local dialect, you can see it in the place names and you can experience it at Up-Helly-Aa, the January fire festival in which a Viking longship – a year in the making – is burned to ashes in a matter of minutes. Boats and the sea are ever-present and together they drive the economy. Among the fishing boats and pleasure craft in Lerwick harbour are oil supply ships, servicing the oilfields in the North Sea and Atlantic. Oil has brought many things to these islands, not least prosperity. If the oil executives underestimated Shetlanders when they began negotiations in the 1970s, they certainly didn't by the time they'd finished. Shetland has used its oil wealth wisely, certainly when it comes to maintaining the road network!

You'll travel a long way before you find somewhere with better country roads than Shetland – even the unclassified ones are pretty free of potholes, and that's not something you can say about the rest of Scotland! The road network spreads out from Lerwick like tentacles on an octopus. Many are dead-ends but, as the views are constantly changing, it's no hardship to return the same way. If you pass a road-end with a Council direction sign pointing into it, try it. In my experience, it's almost always worth exploring, with the likely reward of an attractive bay, interesting jetty or glorious view at the end.

Shetland's main road is the superb A970 which runs from the very top of the mainland to Sumburgh Airport at the south end. From there a single track road extends to the lighthouse at Sumburgh

Head, Shetland's southernmost headland with a view to Fair Isle, 25 miles to the south-west (weather permitting). From there we work our way north, past St Ninian's Isle, through Shetland's ancient capital Scalloway and out to the West Mainland. Then we head north again, crossing the Mavis Grind, a narrow rocky strip which separates the Atlantic from the North Sea. From Eshaness, where Shetland's cliffs are at their most dramatic, we head for the ferry at Toft, passing Sullom Voe Oil Terminal on the way. It's an alien presence in an unspoiled landscape but, as Shetland's cash cow, it's hard to begrudge its presence. A ferry carries us to Yell, and another to Unst, the most northerly inhabited island in the British Isles. It's not the most remote (that title belongs to Foula on Shetland's western extremity) but Unst feels like it's a long, long way from home. As you enjoy a cuppa in Haroldswick, looking across to the bay to a full-sized Viking longship, you are north of Moscow, nearer Norway than Aberdeen and can exercise bragging rights over the lightweights who stop at John O'Groats!

SOUNDTRACK

All Dressed in Yellow by Fiddlers' Bid. A mega-mix from the spiritual home of fiddle music. More power to their elbow!

FURTHER READING

60 Degrees North: Around the World in Search of Home by Malachy Tallack (Pegasus, 2016). Coming to terms with grief; a search for home; the world from a Shetland perspective, this is a travelogue with unusual depth.

TINGWALL VALLEY

WHAT TO SEE:

Museums can be dull and dusty places, but the **Shetland Museum** in Lerwick (ZE1 0WP) is just the opposite. It's an enjoyable shortcut to understanding Shetland's history, culture and traditions. Oil money in action and too good to miss.

Unst Boat Haven in Haroldswick (ZE2 9EQ). A remarkable collection of wooden boats recalling Shetland's fishing history. A tribute to the brave and hardy souls who went far offshore in search of herring. Nearby is the Skidbladner longship, and a replica Viking longhouse beside it.

LOOK OUT FOR

Live music – there's usually something on offer in pubs and venues around the islands. The Lounge Bar in Lerwick has a tune on the go on most weekends. Check *The Shetland Times* for gigs and events.

WHERE TO STAY

Woosung B&B (ZE1 0EN) in Lerwick's St Olaf Street. Central, inexpensive and spotlessly clean.

Almara B&B (ZE2 9RH) near Hillswick. Great place to stay in a lovely setting, with a coin-operated laundry!

The **Sergeants' Mess Hostel** (ZE2 9TP) on the old RAF station at Saxa Vord, Unst, now rebranded as the Saxa Vord Resort. Everything you could want in a hostel, plus bar meals just down the corridor.

WHERE TO EAT

In Lerwick, try the **Fjara Café Bar** (ZE1 0ZJ) on the waterfront behind Tescos, great coffee and an enticing menu.

Sumburgh Head Lighthouse Café (ZE3 9JN) enjoys uninterrupted sea views at the very southern tip of the mainland.

Braewick Café, Eshaness (ZE29 RS). A welcome refreshment after a long road out west.

Victoria's Tearooms in Haroldswick (ZE2 9ED) – a proper tearoom at the end of your journey. Superb!

MUCKLE ROE

SCALLOWAY

1 Turn left from the ferry terminal onto A970 (600 yards)

2 Turn right at roundabout and then follow signs to Sumburgh (25 miles)

3 After rounding the far end of the runway, do not turn left to the terminal building but keep right to follow signs to Sumburgh Head (1.5 miles)

4 Return past airport on A970, through Central Dunrossness (6.5 miles)

5 Turn left onto B9122 to Bigton, to visit St Ninian's Isle (4 miles)

6 Return to T-junction in Bigton and turn right to the B9122 (0.5 miles)

7 Turn left to rejoin the A970 (1.5 miles)

8 Turn left onto A970 (12 miles)

9 Turn left onto B903 following signs to Scalloway (3 miles)

10 Leave Scalloway on the road you arrived by to junction before the quarry (0.5 miles)

11 Turn left, signed Tingwall, to roundabout (3 miles)

12 Turn left to junction (0.5 miles)

13 Turn left onto A971, signed Walls, to Bixter (11 miles)

14 (Continue on A971 to visit Walls and Sandness)

15 As you leave Bixter, turn right onto B9071, to Voe (11 miles)

16 Turn left, onto A970, signed Hillswick (16 miles)

17 Just before reaching Hillswick, turn right onto B9078 to Eshaness (6 miles)

18 Return to Hillswick junction (6 miles)

19 Turn left onto A970 to Brae (3 miles)

20 Turn left onto A970 (10 miles)

21 Turn left onto B9076, signed Sullom Voe Oil Terminal, to T-junction (5 miles)

22 Turn right to T-junction (1.5 miles)

23 Turn left to the Toft ferry terminal (2 miles)

24 Take the ferry

25 Follow the A968 to Gutcher (18 miles)

26 Take the ferry

27 Follow the A968 to Haroldswick (10 miles)

28 Retrace your steps across the two ferries to Toft (29 miles)

29 For an alternative route through Yell, turn left to Mid Yell and follow the road to the ferry

30 Follow the A968 to junction (10 miles)

31 Turn left onto A970 to Lerwick (17 miles)

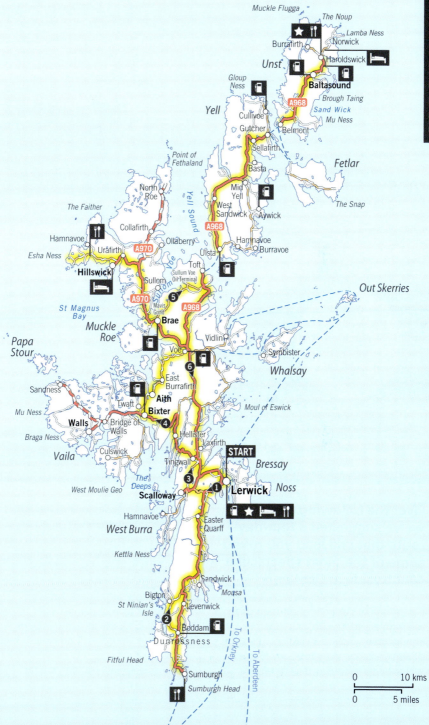

Muckle Flugga

The Noup

★

Burrafirth

Lamba Ness
Norwick

Unst

Haroldswick

Baltasound

Gloup
Ness

Brough Taing

A968

Sand Wick
Mu Ness

Yell

Cullivoe

Gutcher

Belmont

Fetlar

Point of
Fethaland

Sellafirth

Basta

North
Roe

Mid
Yell

Aywick

The Snap

The Faither

Collafirth

West
Sandwick

Out Skerries

Hamnavoe

Urafirth

A970

Ollaberry

Ulsta

Hamnavoe
Burravoe

Esha Ness

Hillswick

Sullom

Toft
Sullum Voe
Oil-Terminal

5

A970

Mavis
Grind

A968

St Magnus
Bay

Brae

**Muckle
Roe**

Vidlin

Papa
Stour

Voe

6

Symbister

Whalsay

East
Burrafirth

Moul of Eswick

Sandness

Twatt

Aith
Bixter

Mu Ness

Walls

Bridge of
Walls

4

Hellister

Laxfirth

START

Braga Ness

Culswick

Tingwall

Bressay

Vaila

The
Deeps

3

1

Lerwick

Noss

West Moulie Geo

Scalloway

Hamnavoe

Easter
Quarff

West Burra

Kettla Ness

Sandwick

Mousa

Bigton

St Ninian's
Isle

Levenwick

2

Boddam

To Orkney

To Aberdeen

Dunrossness

Fitful Head

Sumburgh

Sumburgh Head

0   10 kms

0   5 miles

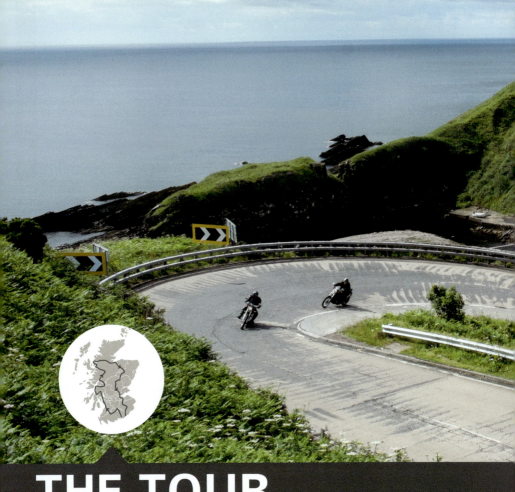

THE TOUR

Over the following pages we've suggested a four-day route that will lead you round some of the most spectacular countryside in Scotland.

Clearly that's not enough time to cover the whole country, but our itinerary should take you within striking distance of every corner. Why four days? Well, this allows readers who only have a week's holiday to factor in travel to and from their homes further south, and still have time to vary the route as they see fit. You might want to head out to Britain's most westerly point at Ardnamurchan, for example, or to spend a day in Edinburgh. For those with more time, the Tour can be used to link routes found elsewhere in this book. For instance, Tour Day 1 passes through Dunoon, from where it is easy to pick up the route to Kintyre, continuing

BERRIEDALE, CAITHNESS

the Tour when you're done. On Day 3, the Tour visits both Applecross and Inverness, allowing you to set off on the NC500 in either a clockwise or anti-clockwise direction.

Most of the routes are easily accessible from the Tour at some point during the four days. We have set a gentle schedule, breaking each day into a morning and afternoon leg. At the same time, we've tried to balance the need to cover the miles with the desire to savour the sights. We've suggested places to stay along each leg of the Tour and we strongly advise booking in advance. Rooms can be hard to find in certain areas, and if you know where you are staying for the night, you can linger longer on the journey without fretting about finding a bed. Take your time, book ahead and be careful!

SCOTLAND TOUR
DAY 1 MORNING
MOFFAT TO IRVINE

TWISTY ▮▮▮▮ STRAIGHTER	**DISTANCE** 106 miles
SINGLE TRACK ▮ WIDER	**ALLOW** 3 hours

LINKS WITH
1 SOLWAY & CARRICK COASTS
2 AROUND THE MERRICK
5 MOFFAT AND SELKIRK LOOP
7 SOUTH LANARKSHIRE CIRCUITS
9 ARRAN

The south-west of Scotland is the country's forgotten corner, by-passed by a motorway that feeds people north as quickly as possible.

THE MENNOCK PASS

As motorways go, the M74 isn't too bad, but it's still a tedious way to put in the miles. So we're taking to the 'service road' that runs beside the motorway, although your progress will probably be just as fast until we head into the Lowther Hills at Elvanfoot. The road takes us through the old mining communities of Leadhills and Wanlockhead (Scotland's highest village), before setting off down a narrow valley. This is the Mennock Pass, popular with local bikers as well as prospectors, who can often be seen panning for gold in the stream. As we make our way down to the valley floor and the hills no longer press in on our flanks, we join the main road to Thornhill. Then we're heading into farming country – stone dykes on either side of the road, fields and forestry beyond, with plenty of varied corners

demanding our concentration. At St John's Town of Dalry, we head north and enjoy more than 25 traffic-free miles of seductive curves and thrilling straights, through the former mining villages of Dalmellington and Patna to the outskirts of Ayr.

Whichever way you choose to reach the Highlands, you have to travel through Scotland's urban sprawl at some point. The next stage is our penance for the fun we've just had… and down payment for the joys that lie ahead! Onto the bypass we go, heading for Glasgow on the A77, but turning towards the coast after passing the huge – but under-used – Prestwick Airport. We're sticking to the coast now, by the Firth of Clyde. To the south is the distinctive profile of Ailsa Craig, with Kintyre and Arran to our left as we

make for the ferry at Gourock. There are plenty of places to stop and eat along the way; our favourite is the café at the Scottish Maritime Museum on the seafront in Irvine.

Our Tour starts from Moffat, a town that has been welcoming travellers since the days of the coach and horse. The main street is lined with old coaching inns, and it's an ideal base from which to begin our exploration of Scotland. To reach Moffat from the M6 northbound (if you have had enough of motorways), turn off at J45 Gretna and go past the retail village. Turn right after crossing above the dual carriageway, and left after passing under the motorway. Now follow the B7076 until you pick up signs to A701 Moffat. It's a lovely alternative to the motorway and almost as quick. It also passes through the wonderfully named village of Ecclefechan, known locally as 'Fechan'. Father Jack impressions come thick and fast as you pass the Fechan Post Office, chat with the Fechan locals and try the local delicacy – a Fechan tart. Chortle, chortle!

SOUNDTRACK

Alive by Skipinnish. Just the thing to put you in the right frame of mind for a motorbike tour of Scotland.

FURTHER READING

A Night Out with Robert Burns by Andrew O'Hagan (Canongate, 2009). Burns's best and most famous poems set out for our enjoyment and given a modern context.

GALLOWAY

WHAT TO SEE

Scotland's favourite poet, Robert Burns, was born in Alloway, just outside Ayr. It's two miles off our route; turn left when you join the A77 (no. 8 opposite) and turn right after one mile to follow signs. The cottage is still standing and there's an impressive **Burns Birthplace Museum** (KA7 4PQ) nearby with exhibitions, shop and a good café.

LOOK OUT FOR

The **road to Loch Doon** on the left-hand side as you head for Dalmellington. There's an enjoyable detour on offer down the side of the water to Loch Doon Castle (KA6 7QE), an eleven-sided keep built either by Robert The Bruce or his father in the 13th century. It used to be on an island in the loch but was moved when they raised the water level in the 1930s.

WHERE TO STAY

The Buccleuch Hotel (DG10 9ET), Moffat. As biker-friendly as it gets and seemingly entirely staffed by bikers.

Lochhouse Farm B&B (DG10 9SG) is a mile and a half from Moffat and close to J15 of the M74. I doubt you'll find better value for money.

WHERE TO EAT

The **Roundhouse by Loch Doon** (KA6 7QE) does a good snack if you take the wee detour before Dalmellington mentioned above.

Puffers Café (KA12 8QG) is on the harbour front in Irvine. It's owned by the nearby Scottish Maritime Museum so you can eat well and help a good cause at the same time.

The Peppermill (KA12 8AX) in Eglington Street, Irvine, does good café food and is very competitively priced, but it's harder to park than at Puffers.

FINISH

START

Galloway Forest Park

Lowther Hills

Clatteringshaws Loch

Loch Doon

River Nith

0	10 kms
0	5 miles

↑ **1** From the centre of Moffat, head downhill on the right-hand side of the street, leaving the town by passing the Esso station (1.5 miles)

↱ **2** Go under the motorway, and at the roundabout take the third exit onto B7076, signed Abington (14 miles)

↰ **3** Shortly after a (fairly pointless) roundabout, turn left onto A702 to Elvanfoot (1 mile)

↦ **4** Turn right onto B7040 and follow signs to Wanlockhead (6 miles)

↑ **5** Continue through Wanlockhead (now on B797) to T-junction (7 miles)

⊤ **6** Turn left onto A76 to Thornhill (10 miles)

↦ **7** At 30mph sign in Thornhill, turn right onto A702 to Moniaive and follow signs to Dalry (21 miles)

↦ **8** Turn right onto A713 to reach the Ayr bypass (31 miles)

↱ **9** Turn right on roundabout onto A77 and follow signs for A78 to Irvine (14 miles)

LOCH DOON

IRVINE TO LOCHGILPHEAD

TWISTY	STRAIGHTER
SINGLE TRACK	WIDER

DISTANCE
97 miles

ALLOW
3.5 hours

LINKS WITH
12 LOCH LOMOND TO GLENCOE
6 KINTYRE

Although there's usually a fine view out over the Firth of Clyde, the road up the north Ayrshire coast is nothing to get excited about, as it passes round or through a series of coastal communities.

But it's not long, and each mile covered brings us nearer the ferry at Gourock. The Western Ferries service to Dunoon is terrific, with two boats running a shuttle service so you don't have to wait long for the 20-minute crossing. Note that it's much cheaper to buy tickets in the town before boarding the ferry. We disembark at Hunter's Quay, just north of Dunoon, and set off along the shore of the Holy Loch, before snaking right and left and turning inland. The road up past Loch Eck is well surfaced, well built and a glorious release after the Ayrshire coast. It's actually the main road from Dunoon to Glasgow, but the traffic tends to use the ferry, leaving the A815 to the likes of you and me. It's a relaxing and rewarding run across the Cowal peninsula to Strachur on Loch Fyne, and then – keeping the loch on

LOCH FYNE

our left – we follow the road along the coast to Inveraray.

Robert Burns wasn't impressed with the place when he visited in 1787, writing: "There's naething here but Highland pride, And Highland scab and hunger; If Providence has sent me here, 'Twas surely in his anger." The poet must have been having a bad day because, by general consent, Inveraray is one of the most attractive coastal towns in Scotland. It was built some 40 years before Burns's visit, by the 3rd Duke of Argyll. The old town of Inveraray was clustered round the castle walls, but the Duke had taken the opportunity, while

having his castle upgraded, of moving the town further away! Originally a fishing village, Inveraray is now pretty much reliant on tourism. If you're camping, call in at Dewar's Boot Store on Main Street (East), where they stock Beaton's midge vests and gloves – well worth the investment as you'll quickly discover when you pitch camp this evening. They also sell Avon's 'Skin So Soft', renowned for it's ability to repel biting insects. Then we continue down the west side of Loch Fyne, passing the entrance to the Crinan Canal at Ardrishaig, to finish the day at Lochgilphead.

SOUNDTRACK

Adore by Heron Valley, who hail from the Cowal Peninsula

FURTHER READING

Para Handy by Neil Munro (Berlinn, 2002). This book of short stories by Inveraray-born Munro recounts the exploits of the skipper and crew of the 'puffer', *Vital Spark*. Steam-powered puffers used to be common around the Clyde and west coast in the days when communities relied on sea transport rather than roads.

INVERARAY

1 From Irvine, rejoin the A78, signed Greenock, to the Bankfoot roundabout, just after Inverkip (approx 30 miles)

2 Turn left on the roundabout onto A770 to Western Ferries Terminal (3 miles)

3 Take the ferry – if you have time, buy tickets before boarding at Paul's Food and Wine (PA19 1RB) two miles further on

4 On disembarking, turn right onto A815, signed Strachur, to T-junction (2 miles)

5 Turn right, continuing on A815 signed to Glasgow, passing through Strachur and to T-junction (25 miles)

6 Turn left onto A83 to Inveraray (11 miles)

7 Continue on A83 to Lochgilphead (25 miles)

WHAT TO SEE

If you like a good looking train station, stop for a wander round the one at **Wemyss Bay** (PA18 6AR). With graceful curves and elegant canopies, it's an Edwardian masterpiece, built not for posh folk but for the working families of Glasgow enjoying a trip "doon the watter" on a steamer from the pier.

Inveraray Jail (PA32 8TX) closed to prisoners in 1889, but reopened as a museum and visitor centre a century later. It's an impressive facility!

LOOK OUT FOR

The turn off (right) onto the B839 a few miles north of Strachur. This offers a lovely detour up the hillside, then down through Hell's Glen to Lochgoilhead. It's 12 miles there and back, single track, complete with hairpin bends.

WHERE TO STAY

The Corran B&B (PA31 8LR) in Lochgilphead has great sea views and off-road parking, and is an easy walk to the local restaurants.

The Horseshoe Inn (PA31 8QA) is four miles beyond Lochgilphead in Bridgend. You pay extra for breakfast, but the rooms are very reasonably priced.

WHERE TO EAT

Sheila's Diner (PA23 8QS) is on the route four miles after disembarking from the ferry. Enjoy a good meal without the tourist prices.

Loch Fyne Oyster Bar (PA26 8BL) offers a seafood experience not to be hurried and probably not to be forgotten. People drive for miles to eat here, and we're passing the door! If you're in a rush (or don't like fish), visit the café in the **Tree Shop Garden Centre** next door.

Brambles Café & Bistro (PA32 8TU) in Inveraray is pretty special. Not the cheapest, but they really make it a worthwhile experience. Breakfasts, lunches, dinners; even take-away if you prefer. They do rooms as well.

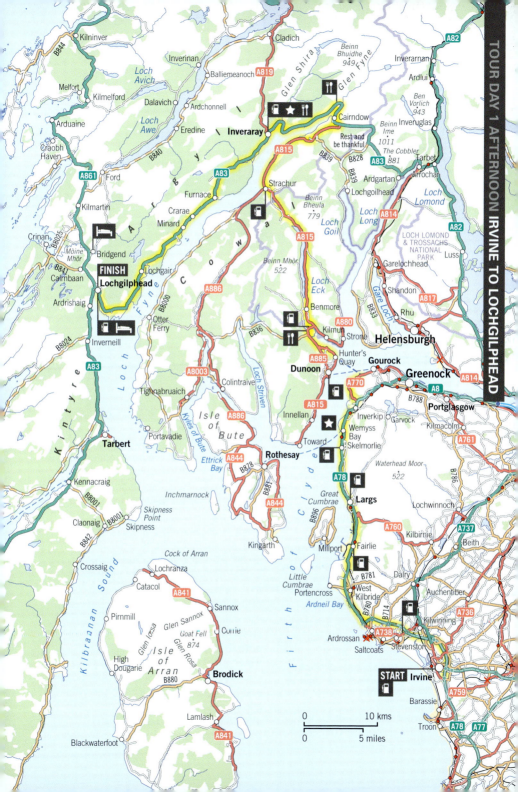

LOCHGILPHEAD TO GLENCOE

| TWISTY | STRAIGHTER |
| SINGLE TRACK | WIDER |

DISTANCE
103 miles

ALLOW
2.5 hours

LINKS WITH
11 TYNDRUM, CRINAN AND SEIL
12 LOCH LOMOND TO GLENCOE
13 MULL
19 THE WESTERN ISLES

Eat a hearty breakfast before setting off because there's a spectacular day ahead, with interest and exhilaration in equal measure.

It begins pretty much from the outset as we skirt the Mòine Mhòr, a vast area of mossy hummocks and raised bog, to Kilmartin, the centre of the ancient kingdom of Dalriada. Then the road becomes something of a roller coaster – dips, rises and corners, some gentle, some almost hairpins – as we make our way up the coast to Oban. The road leads through the centre of the town so it's worth stopping to enjoy the atmosphere around the harbour. Oban is known as the 'gateway to the isles', with ferries operating to half a dozen islands to the west. If you're crossing to Mull, then this is the place to catch the boat. If you have time, climb to McCaig's Tower, the Colosseum-like folly on the hill from where the view is hard to beat.

Back on the road, the Connel Bridge offers the shortest route to Glencoe

RANNOCH MOOR

but, if you take it, you'll miss out on one of Scotland's motorcycling 'crown jewels' – the A82 across Rannoch Moor. To get there, we head under the bridge and follow the road to Tyndrum, where bikers congregate at the Green Welly Stop. Now we're heading uphill, on a sweeping bend, to cross between peaks for a long descent to Bridge of Orchy, and a flat, fast run beside the river to Loch Tulla, where the real drama of this road begins to unfold. First we climb above the loch around the lower slopes of the Black Mount to emerge onto the wide plateau of Rannoch Moor. The landscape is speckled with countless lochs and lochans; peat bogs and burns; high mountains to the west and north; and a vast empty moorland stretching out to the east. This is natural landscape at its most stark and

beautiful, although it's a lot easier to admire in good weather! There will probably be plenty of traffic, but the road is so good that, with care, it's easy and straightforward to overtake when you need to. The moorland comes to an abrupt end by one of Scotland's best known and most photographed mountains, Buachaille Etive Mor, which guards at the entrance to the glen.

The road heads down into the Pass of Glencoe, rocks at your shoulder, vast mountains on either side, before opening out with the full majesty of the glen ahead. Even in poor weather, when clouds shroud the hills, this place has an allure quite unlike anywhere else in Scotland…simply awe-inspiring. Just past the loch is the site of the infamous 1692 massacre, when soldiers – led by

a Campbell – attempted to wipe out the MacDonalds. It's a beautiful spot, but it retains an air of melancholy to this day. If you're called Campbell, best not stop!

SOUNDTRACK

Rattle of a Simple Man by The Humpff Family.

FURTHER READING

In Search of Scotland by H.V. Morton (Methuen, 2000). A genial travelogue through 1920s Scotland written by a journalist who not only witnessed the Atlantic Treaty meeting between Roosevelt and Churchill, but was also present at the opening of Tutankhamen's tomb by Howard Carter.

PASSING BEINN DORAIN ON THE A82

From Lochgilphead:

1 Turn right onto A816 to Oban (37 miles)

2 Put the sea on your left to leave Oban on the A85, signed Crianlarich, to T-junction (36 miles)
Note: Tyndrum is a short detour to your right

4 Turn left onto A82, signed Fort William, to Glencoe (30 miles)

WHAT TO SEE

The spot in **Glen Etive** (PH49 4JA) where Judi Dench and Daniel Craig stood side by side in the 2012 Bond movie, *Skyfall*. From the A82, it's the first turning on the left after the Glencoe Mountain Resort.

LOOK OUT FOR

Deer! They have a habit of wandering onto the A82, particularly in the early morning or late evening.

Speed Traps. The A82 across Rannoch Moor is a favourite spot for the police to catch speeding bikers and motorists. They use unmarked police cars and bikes as well.

WHERE TO STAY

Clachaig Inn (PH49 4HX), Glencoe. Close to the site of the massacre, the Clachaig has been around for centuries, providing shelter and refreshment for walkers, climbers and anyone who is passing. For as long as anyone can remember, there's been a sign at the front desk, saying: 'No Hawkers, No Campbells.' From time to time there are suggestions that they should let hawkers in.

WHERE TO EAT

The Oban Seafood Hut (PA34 4DB) on the ferry pier. Its fame has spread far and wide, so you may have to queue.

The Green Welly Stop (FK20 8RY) in Tyndrum for coffee, food, petrol, gifts and a dedicated bike parking area. Or the **Real Food Café** across the road, which is smaller and quieter.

For an evening meal in Glencoe, eat at the **Clachaig**, or head along the road to **The Laroch** restaurant (PH49 4JB) in Ballachulish.

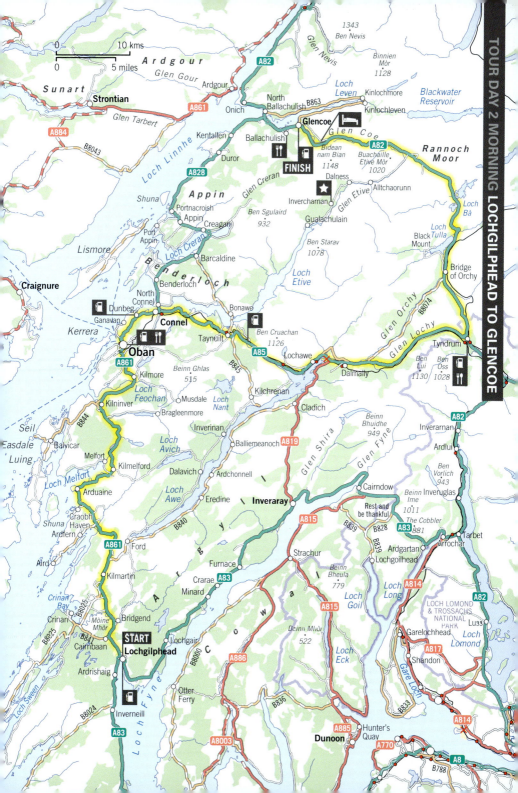

Ardgour

Sunart

Strontian

A861

A884

B8043

Glen Gour

Ardgour

Onich

North
Ballachulish

B863

Kentallen

Ballachulish

Duror

FINISH

Glencoe

Glen Coe

A82

Bidean
nam Bian
1148

Dalness

Invercharnan

Gualachulain

Glen Etive

Glen Tarbert

Loch Linnhe

A828

A82

Glen Nevis

1343
Ben Nevis

Binnien
Mòr
1128

Loch
Leven

Kinlochmore

Kinlochleven

Blackwater
Reservoir

Buachaille
Etive Mòr
1020

Rannoch
Moor

Loch
Bà

Loch
Tulla

Black
Mount

Bridge
of Orchy

Shuna

Appin

Portnacroish

Appin

Creagan

Port
Appin

Lismore

Craignure

Benderloch

Glen Creran

Ben Sgulaird
932

Loch Creran

Barcaldine

North
Connel

Dunbeg

Ganavan

Kerrera

Connel

Oban

A861

Kilmore

Beinn Ghlas
515

Benderloch

Bonawe

Taynuilt

Ben Cruachan
1126

Lochawe

Dalmally

A85

Loch
Etive

Ben Starav
1078

Glen Orchy

B8074

Glen Lochy

Tyndrum

Ben
Lui
1130

Ben
Oss
1028

Seil

Easdale

Luing

Loch
Feochan

Kilninver

Balvicar

Musdale

Bragleenmore

Loch
Nant

Kilchrenan

Cladich

Inverinan

Melfort

Loch
Avich

Kilmelford

Dalavich

Ardchonnell

B844

B840

Loch
Melfort

Arduaine

Craobh
Haven

Shuna

Ardfern

Aird

A861

Eredine

Loch
Awe

Ford

Balliemeanoch

A819

Inveraray

Glen Shira

Beinn
Bhuidhe
949

Glen Fyne

Beinn Ime
1011

Inverarnan

Ardlui

Ben
Vorlich
943

Inveruglas

The Cobbler
881

A83

Cairndow

Rest and
be thankful

A815

B839

B828

Tarbet

Arrochar

Ardgartan

Lochgoilhead

Crinan
Bay

Crinan

B8025

Cairnbaan

Môine
Mhòr

B841

Bridgend

Kilmartin

Lochgair

START
Lochgilphead

Ardrishaig

Inverneill

A83

Furnace

Crarae

Minard

A83

B8000

A886

Strachur

Beinn
Bheula
779

Deinn Mhòr
522

Loch
Goil

A815

A814

Loch
Long

Garelochhead

A817

Shandon

LOCH LOMOND
& TROSSACHS
NATIONAL
PARK

Luss

A82

Loch
Lomond

Loch
Eck

A8003

Otter
Ferry

B8024

B8836

Dunoon

A885

Hunter's
Quay

A770

Gare Loch

B833

A814

A8

B788

LOCH LEVEN

TWISTY   STRAIGHTER

SINGLE TRACK   WIDER

 DISTANCE
103 miles

 ALLOW
2.5 hours

LINKS WITH
18 THE GREAT GLEN
20 INVERGARRY TO SKYE
24 APPLECROSS AND LOCH EWE

Ballachulish sits at the mouth of Loch Leven and, in the days when a ferry operated across the narrows, it used to be a dreadful bottleneck on the way to Fort William.

Vehicles queued back towards Glencoe, with marker posts informing drivers, 'Thirty minutes if queuing from here.' Two marker posts and it was quicker to take a 16-mile detour round by Kinlochleven. Nowadays, although the steel bridge will carry us swiftly across the water, the road round the loch makes an attractive alternative for those not in a rush. From the north end of the bridge, it's a bit of a slog – heavy traffic, speed restrictions and double white lines can sap the joy out of the 12 miles beside Loch Linnhe, but it's soon over. On quick inspection, Fort William will probably disappoint the first-time visitor, but it is the gateway to the magnificent roads that lie to the north and west. As we leave the town, it's hard to resist the temptation to nip along to Glenfinnan. The well-signposted, 30-mile round trip leads to the monument where Bonnie Prince Charlie began the second Jacobite uprising, as well as to the viaduct made famous by the Harry Potter films.

Then we head up 'The Great Glen', making for Spean Bridge and the Commando Memorial that honours the troops who trained nearby during the Second World War. Loch Lochy is on our left, then Loch Oich on our right until we turn west at Invergarry. The A87 is another of Scotland's 'must ride' roads, threading its way through

the mountains – snow-capped in early spring or late autumn – before diving down to Eilean Donan Castle. We leave the A87 before the Skye Bridge, sweeping round a glorious right-hander as we climb into the hills. The road is laid out across the landscape – sometimes cut through rock for a straighter line – until Loch Carron stretches before us and, from the viewpoint, Stromeferry sits below. Our day's final destination is now in sight on the other side of the loch and we drop down to the water's edge, separated from the sea only by a railway line. Two right turns and we've arrived in Lochcarron. If Skye is on your list of

places to visit on the tour, don't turn right at Direction 6, just continue ahead to cross the Skye Bridge.

SOUNDTRACK

Lochaber No More – written by Allan Ramsay in the early 19th century but sung by Breabach a lot more recently.

FURTHER READING

Commandos: The Definitive History of Commando Operations in the Second World War by Charles Messenger (William Collins, 2016)

EILEAN DONAN CASTLE

1 From Glencoe, turn right after the filling station, onto B863 to Kinlochleven. Continue along the other side of the loch to rejoin A82 at North Ballachulish (16 miles)

2 Turn right onto A82 to Fort William (12 miles)

3 Continue on A82, signed Inverness, to Invergarry (24 miles)

4 Turn left onto A87, signed Kyle of Lochalsh, to Eilean Donan Castle (41 miles)

5 Continue on A87 to junction with A890 (3 miles)

6 Turn right onto A890 over level-crossing to T-junction (15 miles)

7 Turn left onto A896 (2.5 miles)

WHAT TO SEE

Lochaber from on high. Cable cars run up the side of Aonach Mor, giving superb views out over the mountains and lochs (fees apply). It was built for skiers but is just as busy in the summer with walkers, climbers and lazy sods wanting to enjoy the view without putting in the effort. Look for the brown sign to 'Nevis Range' (PH33 6SQ), just north of Fort William on the A82.

LOOK OUT FOR

The **Jacobite steam train** that operates between Fort William and Mallaig. It's a great sight anywhere along the line, but best seen as it crosses the **Glenfinnan Viaduct** (PH37 4LT).

WHERE TO STAY

The Sithean (IV54 8YH) provides good B&B at pretty much the standard rate around Lochcarron – it's pronounced 'She'un'. Or try the **Loch Dubh** (IV54 8YA), pronounced 'Loch Doo'. Don't leave your accommodation in this part of the world to chance – booking ahead is essential.

WHERE TO EAT

For an evening meal in Lochcarron, treat yourself at the **Lochcarron Bistro** (IV54 8YB). It's not the cheapest place on the west coast, but you won't go to bed hungry. Or continue along the road a few miles to the **Kishorn Seafood Bar** (IV54 8XA), a classy 'shack' by the roadside, which serves the freshest seafood with little fuss. Superb!

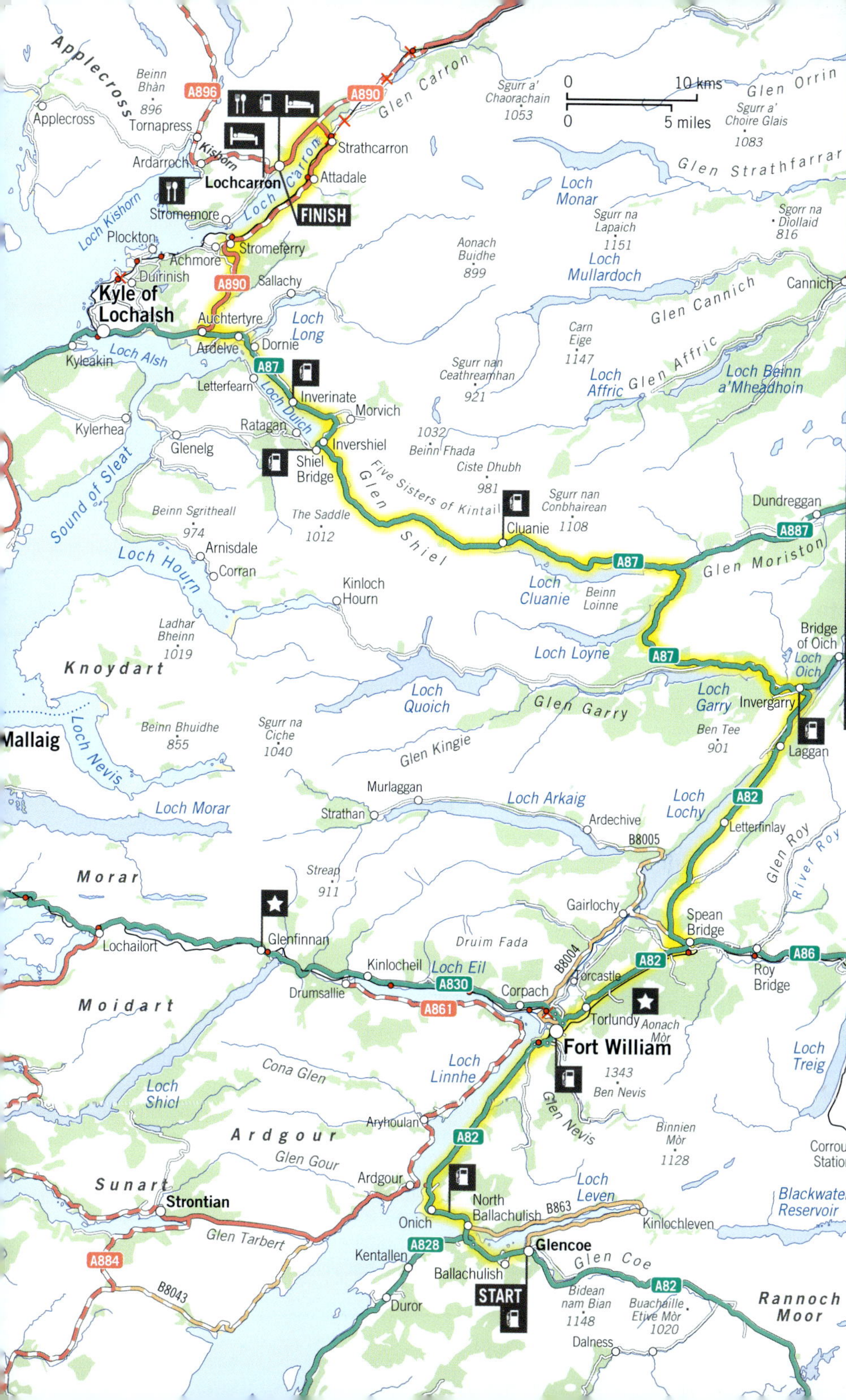
0
10 kms
0
5 miles
FINISH
START
Applecross
Beinn Bhàn 896
Tornapress
A896
A890
Glen Carron
Sgurr a' Chaorachain 1053
Glen Orrin
Sgurr a' Choire Glais 1083
Kishorn
Ardarroch
Lochcarron
Strathcarron
Attadale
Loch Carron
Stromemore
Loch Kishorn
Plockton
Stromeferry
Achmore
Duirinish
Kyle of Lochalsh
Sallachy
Auchtertyre
Ardelve
Dornie
Loch Long
Kyleakin
Loch Alsh
A87
Letterfearn
Loch Duich
Inverinate
Morvich
Kylerhea
Ratagan
Inversheil
Glenelg
Shiel Bridge
Sound of Sleat
Loch Monar
Sgurr na Lapaich 1151
Loch Mullardoch
Glen Strathfarrar
Sgorr na Diollaid 816
Aonach Buidhe 899
Cannich
Glen Cannich
Carn Eige 1147
Sgurr nan Ceathreamhan 921
Loch Affric
Glen Affric
Loch Beinn a'Mheadhoin
1032
Beinn Fhada
Ciste Dhubh 981
Five Sisters of Kintail
Glen Shiel
Sgurr nan Conbhairean 1108
Cluanie
Dundreggan
A887
Beinn Sgritheall 974
The Saddle 1012
Arnisdale
Corran
Loch Hourn
Kinloch Hourn
Loch Cluanie
Beinn Loinne
Glen Moriston
Ladhar Bheinn 1019
Knoydart
Loch Loyne
Bridge of Oich
Loch Oich
Loch Quoich
Glen Garry
Loch Garry
Invergarry
Mallaig
Loch Nevis
Beinn Bhuidhe 855
Sgurr na Ciche 1040
Glen Kingie
Ben Tee 901
Laggan
A82
Murlaggan
Strathan
Loch Arkaig
Loch Lochy
Ardechive
Letterfinlay
Loch Morar
B8005
Glen Roy
River Roy
Morar
Streap 911
Gairlochy
Spean Bridge
Lochailort
Glenfinnan
Druim Fada
Roy Bridge
A86
Kinlocheil
Loch Eil
B8004
Torcastle
A830
Drumsallie
Corpach
Moidart
A861
Torlundy
Aonach Mòr
Fort William
Cona Glen
Loch Linnhe
1343
Ben Nevis
Loch Treig
Loch Shiel
Glen Nevis
Aryhoulan
Ardgour
Binnien Mòr 1128
Corrour Station
Glen Gour
Ardgour
Sunart
Loch Leven
Blackwater Reservoir
Strontian
North Ballachulish
B863
Onich
Kinlochleven
Glen Tarbert
A828
Glencoe
Kentallen
Glen Coe
A884
Ballachulish
B8043
Bidean nam Bian 1148
Buachaille Etive Mòr 1020
Rannoch Moor
Duror
Dalness

DAY 3 MORNING
LOCHCARRON TO INVERNESS

TWISTY	STRAIGHTER
SINGLE TRACK	WIDER

DISTANCE
111 miles

ALLOW
3.5 hours

LINKS WITH
23 NC500
25 THE BLACK ISLE AND STRATH BRORA

THE BEALACH NA BÀ

Unless you really want a long lie, set your alarm for an early start in the morning.

It's only a few miles from Lochcarron to the top of Bealach na Bà, the old drover's road that translates from Gaelic as 'Pass of the Cattle'. You can easily be there and back in time for breakfast. It's a climb of over 2,000 feet on one of the most dramatic roads in the country – single track, with hairpin bends as you approach the summit, through a wild and unspoilt landscape. If you get a chance to look back over Loch Kishorn, the view is outstanding and, once you've reached the top, there's a panorama taking in Wester Ross, Skye, Rum and the Outer Hebrides… weather permitting, of course! There's so much to take in and yet, if there's traffic about, the road demands your attention. That's why an early start is recommended. Do it before the rest of the world is awake, and you can enjoy the views and the road at the same time. And if you head back for breakfast, you can do it again. This is a 'bucket list' road for many people and attracts bikers, classic car enthusiasts and camper-vans, although it's not for the faint-hearted!

It's not so long ago that this was the only road to Applecross. As we head north from the village, hugging the shore, we pass an MOD base at Sand Bay – something to do with testing torpedoes, we're told – which was the catalyst for the new road being built in 1975. And what a lovely road it is; quite different from the high pass, it runs straight across the coastal grassland, Raasay and then Rona to our left, before we undulate round the northern tip of the peninsula. Before long, glimpses of

the Torridon mountains appear ahead and we're twisting our way above the loch to Shieldaig, almost in the water as we approach the village. The single track continues up Glen Torridon – high peaks on either side – to Kinlochewe, where we join the wider, faster road heading east, still among the mountains but no longer hindered by traffic. The road is straight and smooth, high gears all the way, as the rocky peaks gradually give way to rolling hills and finally to low-lying farmland for the run into Inverness. The last few miles are on a dual carriageway, arriving in Inverness over the spectacular Kessock Bridge.

SOUNDTRACK

Music Tree by Heidi Talbot. Press 'play' as you turn away from the sea into the Bealach and let the *Music Tree* carry you to the viewing point.

FURTHER READING

Calum's Road by Roger Hutchinson (Birlinn, 2008). The true story of Calum McLeod's efforts to attract people to the north end of Raasay where he was the only inhabitant. When the council wouldn't build a road, he did it himself.

COAST ROAD, APPLECROSS

WHAT TO SEE

Two stunning viewpoints. First at the top of the **Bealach na Bà** for a view out over to Skye. Secondly, in **Glen Docherty**, 3 miles after Kinlochewe (Direction No.5) on the A832. The view is the cover shot for this book. If you're lucky, you might spot a leaping salmon at the **Falls of Rogie**. A suspension bridge provides a wonderful view of the waterfalls and surrounding woodland. To have any chance of catching a glimpse of salmon trying to get upstream to spawn, you have to be there between July and September. And the river level needs to be fairly high. Even then it's a fairly rare sight these days, although the Falls are worth seeing in their own right. The car park (IV14 9EQ) is well signed from the A835, some four miles after Garve. It's a 200-yard walk to the Falls.

LOOK OUT FOR

Inverness Caledonian Thistle Football Club's stadium on the left after crossing the Kessock Bridge (IV1 1FB). Without 'Caley', as the club is known, the world would never have had the best newspaper headline of all time, written when they beat Celtic 3-1 in 2000 to win the Scottish Cup. Google it. Genius!

WHERE TO STAY

It has to be **Torguish House** (IV2 5XQ), just off the A9, five miles south of Inverness. Well known in biker circles, run by bikers and 100% biker-friendly.

WHERE TO EAT

Whistle Stop Café (IV22 2PF), Kinlochewe. Delightful!

Tarvie Services (IV14 9EJ), between Garve and Contin. Free of frills, but good food 'for the road' at sensible prices.

Inverness is full of places. For a quick bite, try the **Grumpy Chef** (IV1 1NA) on Chapel Street. Superb menu. It's a takeaway, but there's a bench outside.

0   10 kms
0   5 miles

Lairg

River Oykel

Bonar Bridge

River Carron

Ullapool

Laide

Autbea

B8057   B8021

Poolewe

Gairloch

B8056

An Teallach
1082

Fionn
Loch

A832

Beinn
Dearg
1081

A835

Loch Broom

Loch Maree

Slioch
980

Sgurr
Mor
1093

Loch
Fannich

Ben
Wyvis
1046

B9176

Alness

A9

Cromarty Firth

B9163
B9160

Cromarty

A832

Fortrose

Moray Firth

B9099
B9092

Rona

A832

Torridon

Beinn Eighe
1010

Kinlochewe

A832

Achnasheen

Garve

Dingwall

A834

Contin

A862

Muir of Ord
Beauly

A832

Tore

A96

B3006

Inner Sound

Applecross

Shieldaig

Torridon

A896

A890

Loch Monar

A831

River Glass

River Farran

FINISH

INVERNESS

A861
B851

Applecross

Lochcarron

START

Loch
Carron

A833

A82

Raasay

Scalpay

A890

A87

Kyle of Lochalsh

A851

A87

Kintail
Five Sisters

A87

Loch
Mullardoch

Carn Eige
1147

Loch Affric

Loch
Cluanie

Cannich

A831

Drumnadrochit

River Moriston

Invermoriston

A887

Loch Ness

B862

B851

River Findhorn

Monadhliath Mountains

Fort
Augustus

↑ **1** In Lochcarron, put the water to your left and follow the A896 towards Shieldaig (7 miles)

↰ **2** Just before the Bealach Café & Gallery turn left onto unclassified road to Applecross (11 miles)

↱ **3** At T-junction in Applecross, turn right, signed Shieldaig (25 miles)

↰ **4** Turn left at T-junction onto A896, signed Kinlochewe (18 miles)

↱ **5** Turn right onto A832, signed Inverness, to T-junction (25 miles)

↱ **6** Turn right onto A835 and follow signs to Inverness (25 miles)

GLEN DOCHERTY

INVERNESS TO PITLOCHRY

TWISTY	STRAIGHTER
SINGLE TRACK	WIDER

 DISTANCE
125 miles

 ALLOW
3.5 hours

LINKS WITH
21 SPEYSIDE TO BANFF
17 AROUND THE CAIRNGORMS
15 THE ANGUS GLENS

GAIRNSHIEL BRIDGE

This afternoon begins where it all ended for the Jacobites – Culloden.

There's no better place to learn about the 1745 rebellion and its cruel aftermath than the impressive visitor centre beside the battlefield. Soon after, a detour northward offers a chance to visit Fort George, the awe-inspiring fortress built in the years after the battle and which, although still operational as an army barracks, appears to have changed little over the centuries. The road that the army built to the fort has become another of Scotland's legendary biking roads, leading us first through Grantown-on-Spey and Tomintoul. Then we're climbing – the tarmac stretching into the distance – over the top of the Lecht and descending, with hardly a house in sight, to Cock Bridge. We cross Gairnshiel Bridge, a simple rubble arch that was built for the army in 1751, and yet is able to carry today's heavy goods vehicles without complaint. Soon we descend into Royal Deeside, close to the Royal Family's Highland retreat at Balmoral for the run into Braemar.

In many ways, the best is yet to come as we set off down the A93, still following the route of the old military road but on a modern surface that could have been set down for the pleasure of the motorcyclist. We soar past the ski resort – our second of the day – and then drop down to Spittal of Glenshee, the modern road by-passing the old settlement and the burned out remains of a local hotel. It's less straight now as we weave along the valley floor, the surface rising and falling as we lean into left- and right-hand bends until

we turn right for Pitlochry. Another section of river valley follows until we're back on the high ground, across the heather moor to the Tay Valley and the wonderful descent through Moulin and into the pretty, bustling Victorian town of Pitlochry. It will seem like a different world to the isolation of the afternoon's motorcycling.

SOUNDTRACK

Happy Place by Ross Ainslie

FURTHER READING

Life and Death of a Highland Hotel by James Carron (Armenta Publishing, 2017). A photographic record of a hotel that burned down in 2014, ending a tradition of refuge and hospitality that had existed in Spittal of Glenshee for over a thousand years. It was (at least) the second hotel there to burn down – and the charred remains have yet to be cleared away.

GLEN SHEE

1 Leave Inverness by following signs to A9, and head south, signed Perth

2 One mile south of Raigmore interchange (A96 to Aberdeen turn off), bear left onto slip road, signed Culloden, to T-junction (200 yards)

3 Turn right onto B9006 to Culloden battlefield site (4 miles)

4 Continue on B9006 to Clephanton (6 miles). *[To visit Fort George, turn left at Clephanton crossroads and follow signs. The fort is five miles to the north]*

5 Turn right onto B9090, to Cawdor and on to T-junction (6 miles)

6 Turn right onto A939 to Grantown-on-Spey (21 miles)

7 At traffic lights turn left, following signs to Tomintoul (14 miles)

8 Turn left on A939, following signs to Braemar A93 (32 miles)

9 Continue on A93 through Spittal of Glenshee to road junction (23 miles)

10 Turn right, and follow signs to Pitlochry (16 miles)

WHAT TO SEE

Braemar Castle (AB35 5XR) is right beside the road half a mile north of Braemar itself. It dates from 1628 and is a great opportunity to see a Scottish tower house close up.

LOOK OUT FOR

The road into **Edradour Distillery** (PH16 5JP), as you come down the hill towards Pitlochry. Edradour is Scotland's last 'farm' distillery still in production. If you haven't visited a whisky distillery during your visit to Scotland so far, Edradour is a fine example.

WHERE TO STAY

Silverhowe B&B (PH16 5LY) in Pitlochry. On the edge of town, offering secure bike parking and clothes-drying facilities.

WHERE TO EAT

The **Bridge of Brown Tearoom** (AB37 9HR) has a slightly uninspiring exterior, but don't let that put you off.

The Gathering Place (AB35 5YP) in Braemar is in a good location, has a decent menu and is just across the road from the **Hungry Highlander**, if you decide you'd rather have fish & chips.

There are over 20 places to eat in Pitlochry's main street and another seems to open (or close) each week. The **Escape Route Café** is first rate, **The Old Mill** is a good bet, as is **The Auld Smiddy**. Or try the **Visitor Centre at the Dam** (PH16 5FG) – harder to find, but it's a spectacular spot, and full of interest.

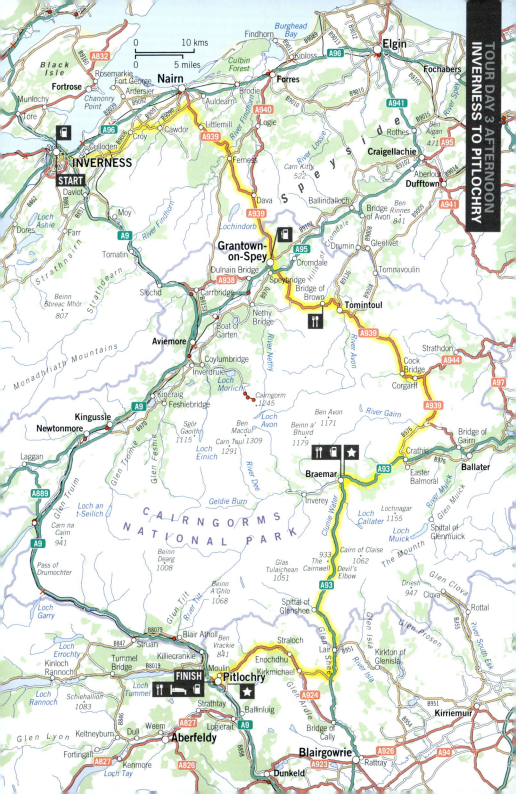

DAY 4 MORNING
PITLOCHRY TO PEEBLES

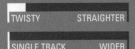

TWISTY	STRAIGHTER
SINGLE TRACK	WIDER

DISTANCE
122 miles

ALLOW
3.5 hours

LINKS WITH
14 RANNOCH AND GLEN LYON
4 HAWICK, DAWYCK AND HERMITAGE CASTLE

THE FIRTH OF FORTH

This morning's itinerary includes a 25-mile section of urban motoring, which we can't really avoid as we make out way south.

The roads from Dunfermline to the south side of Edinburgh include some motorway – delightfully punctuated by the new crossing over the Firth of Forth – and the rather dreary Edinburgh bypass. It's a shame, but it doesn't last long and there are some wonderful routes either side to make up for it.

We start in some of Scotland's most enchanting countryside as we cross the Garry Bridge into the Tummel Valley. The road is a convoluted affair, twisting its way round every bulge in the hillside, with ancient trees obscuring the view but never spoiling the enjoyment. The loch comes into view for a few hundred yards as we pass Strath Tummel (just an inn and a few houses), before we're back among trees and making for Loch Tummel. A left turn takes us on an old military road, single track but wide enough to pass oncoming cars with ease, as we climb steeply to the summit and down the other side. The road passes Dull, famously twinned with Boring in Oregon and now also aligned with Bland in New South Wales! We arrive in Aberfeldy via the most extravagant of all the 18th-century military bridges, this one complete with decorative parapets and obelisks.

The road south takes us over the moorland to the Sma' Glen, a sort of pocket-sized Glencoe, where the Romans chose to build a fort. Later, the producers of the film *Chariots of Fire* chose it as the location for the Highland

Games scene where we are introduced to Eric Liddell. From here it's a smooth, flowing road to Crieff – once the meeting point for most of the Highland drove roads – and on through the south Perthshire countryside to Scotland's former capital of Dunformline. The motorway takes us on the Queensferry Crossing over the Firth of Forth and onto the Edinburgh by-pass, before we are released onto quieter roads for the gentle run to Peebles.

SOUNDTRACK

Wet Field Day by The Elephant Sessions

FURTHER READING

The Briggers: The Story of the Men Who Built the Forth Bridge by Elspeth Wills (Birlinn, 2009). Building giant bridges was a different game back in 1890. *The Briggers* shows how it was done and the human cost of doing it.

WHAT TO SEE

The Scottish Vintage Bus Museum (KY12 0SJ) is a mile off the road as you head for Dunfermline, in the grandly named 'M90 Commerce Park'. If you're under 100, there's a bus from your childhood in the collection – over 160 of them at the last count. There's a small sign to the Commerce Park roughly three miles after passing Knockhill Racetrack.

The Kelpies (FK2 7ZT). Impressive, 100-foot steel statues of horse's heads rising from the ground. It's a 16-mile detour (each way) but worth it, especially if you then follow signs to the **Falkirk Wheel** (FK1 4RS), a unique rotating lift which transfers boats between canals. To visit, follow signs to M9 Stirling after you cross the River Forth, leaving at J5 to follow signs to Helix Park and The Kelpies, also picking up signs to The Falkirk Wheel.

The Great Polish Map of Scotland (EH45 8QW) is a few miles north Peebles in the grounds of the Barony Castle Hotel. A massive relief map of Scotland built in the 1970s, it serves as an impressive 3D reminder Scotland's hospitality to Polish forces in the war, and a powerful symbol of the Polish role in protecting Scotland from invasion in wartime. Recently restored and surrounded by water again, it's a concrete masterpiece. Park at the hotel and walk to the left of the building.

LOOK OUT FOR

Low-flying military aircraft as you make your way from Tummel Bridge to Aberfeldy. Impressive if you see them coming, disconcerting if they overtake you from behind!

Knockhill – our route passes Scotland's premier racetrack. Google Knockhill and check the website for dates.

WHERE TO STAY

Galvelbeg House Guesthouse (PH7 3EQ) is a good choice if you want to stay in Crieff. It has a variety of rooms and off-road parking, does a terrific breakfast and the prices are lower than you might expect. It's on the Perth Road as you enter the town.

The Leadburn Inn (EH46 7BE) is a popular stop for bikers. The rooms are comfortable and clean and it's an easy run into Edinburgh if you want to visit the capital. Stay on the first Thursday of the month and you'll find the place inundated with bikers meeting for the regular 'Thunder Thursdays'.

WHERE TO EAT

Highland Safaris (PH15 2JQ) in Dull has an excellent café and doesn't charge the earth either. You might be tempted to take a Land Rover safari up into the hills while you're there.

The Crieff Food Co (PH7 3HU) features a flash deli upstairs and a decent eatery downstairs. Not your usual biker's caff, but it's healthy, wholesome and a surprising find in the centre of town.

Biker's Cove (EH30 9TB) is tucked under the southern end of the Forth Rail Bridge. It's a little off the route, the food is basic (to say the least), the coffee is instant and the seating is al fresco... but it has a leather-clad charm about it. Very friendly, and there are always a few bikers ready to strike up a conversation.

Or **The Down The Hatch Café** (EH30 9SQ) in the Port Edgar boatyard under the old Forth Road Bridge. Possibly the best Full Scottish breakfast in the country and it's served in the skillet! Seek out the toilets (it's a bit of a walk) for a great view of the three most famous Forth Bridges.

THE KELPIES

THE SMA' GLEN

1 In Pitlochry's main street, put Fishers Hotel on your left and follow the road out of town

2 Continue ahead onto B8019 to the Garry Bridge turning (2.5 miles)

3 Turn left, still on B8019, signed Tummel Bridge (11 miles)

4 Turn left onto B846 to Aberfeldy (13 miles)

5 Ahead at the traffic lights onto A826, and follow signs to Crieff (23 miles)

6 Continue through Crieff high street until give way sign at crossroads

7 Turn left onto A822, signed Stirling, passing through Muthill to road junction (5 miles)

8 Turn left onto A823 and follow signs to Dunfermline (26 miles)

9 Bear left at traffic lights onto Carnegie Drive (500 yards)

10 Turn right at roundabout following signs to join M90 (3 miles)

11 On slip road, follow signs to M90(S) Edinburgh, to cross the Firth of Forth (3 miles)

12 Continue on M90, to J1A (5 miles)

13 Bear left onto M9, following signs to A8 Airport (1 mile)

14 Bear left onto A8, past the airport to pick up signs to City By-Pass (3 miles)

15 Keep left of underpass to join a roundabout and turn right, onto City By-Pass (500 yards)

16 Continue on City By-Pass, leaving at the exit for Carlisle A702 (6 miles)

17 Turn right to cross over the by-pass, signed Penicuik (0.5 miles)

18 Soon after passing a petrol station, turn left onto A703 to Penicuik. (NB There are two roads on the left in quick succession. Make sure to take the second of them) (5 miles)

19 Continue through Penicuik, following signs to Peebles (13 miles)

SCOTLAND TOUR
DAY 4 AFTERNOON
PEEBLES TO LONGTOWN

LANGHOLM

TWISTY — STRAIGHTER	**DISTANCE** 92 miles	
SINGLE TRACK — WIDER	**ALLOW** 2.5 hours	

LINKS WITH
4 HAWICK, DAWYCK AND HERMITAGE CASTLE
5 MOFFAT AND SELKIRK
7 SOUTH LANARKSHIRE
8 HADDINGTON TO HAWICK
3 RIDING THE MARCHES

The final leg takes us back to the border along (arguably) the most enjoyable of the old highways between Scotland and England.

The A7 doesn't have the most dramatic of border crossings – that can be found on the A68 to the east – but it passes through wonderful countryside, has flowing bends and sports a decent surface. It's probably the quietest road in the country to be officially designated a 'trunk road'. If you do find yourself in traffic, there are overtaking opportunities around most corners.

The A7's route through the soft, rolling hills of the Borders has been largely unchanged for decades, so it runs through the bustling towns of Selkirk and Hawick where busier highways would surely have led to the creation of bypasses. However, these are Border towns, not urban sprawls, and their presence on our route only adds to the interest. Before we join the A7, and to remind ourselves that the holiday

is not over yet, we have a few miles of thrilling single track road to follow, carrying us from one reservoir to the next as we take the long, enjoyable way round to Selkirk.

Now we're on the A7, joining it in Selkirk's Market Place to climb out of the town, heading for Hawick, on a fast road with sweeping corners. South of Hawick the road degrades a little but it's still a fabulous run in a narrow valley following the River Teviot south, over the watershed, and down to join the River Esk at Langholm. It's hard to believe this is one of the trunk roads between Scotland and England. We stay close to the river bank as we cross the border south of Canonbie and head into Longtown.

Your tour of Scotland may be over but there are plenty of terrific options to carry you south, depending on where

you are headed: you could make for the Lake District via Carlisle; or follow signs for Brampton, Alston and then Barnard Castle for the most uplifting way to the A1. If you're heading for Newcastle (and the ferry at North Shields), leave the A69 where it becomes a short section of dual carriageway and follow signs to Chollerford. The old road by Hadrian's Wall is superb, with much to see along the way. From Chollerford, follow signs to Newcastle.

If you plan to take the M6 as a quick way south, you can delay the misery for a while yet. Consider its predecessor, the A6, which shadows the motorway for the first 30 miles to Penrith and Shap. It's a lovely road and a perfectly viable alternative. Leave the M6 at J42, that's the second junction after joining from Longtown, and follow the signs. Rejoin the M6 by turning left after Shap.

There are plenty of magnificent roads in the north of England to enjoy and explore before you are back among the crowds further south. Haste ye back!

SOUNDTRACK

Haste Ye Back by Andy Stewart, seamlessly followed by *Auld Lang Syne* by Die Toten Hosen.

FURTHER READING

Scotland by Colin Baxter (Colin Baxter Photography, 2017) will serve as stunning visual memento of your trip round the country. For the other side of the coin, *This is Scotland: A Country in Words and Pictures* by Daniel Gray and Alan McCredie (Luath Press, 2014). As the authors warn you at the start, *"this is not the Scotland as the brochures display it. This is… a nation of beautiful, haggard normality."*

THE A701

↑ **1** Leave Peebles on A72, signed Glasgow, to junction with B712 (4 miles)

↵ **2** Turn left onto B712, signed Stobo/Drumelzier, to T-junction (7 miles)

↰ **3** Turn left onto A701, signed Moffat, to Talla turn off (7 miles)

↵ **4** Turn left onto unclassified road, signed Talla/Fruid, to T-junction (12 miles)

↵ **5** Turn left onto A708 to Selkirk, following signs to town centre (17 miles)

↑ **6** Continue ahead onto A7 turning right to Hawick (11 miles)

↱ **7** Turn right at roundabout following signs to A7 Carlisle, to Langholm (23 miles)

↑ **8** Continue on A7 to Longtown (11 miles)

WHAT TO SEE

Traquair House (EH44 6PW) is the oldest continuously inhabited house in Scotland. Built in 1107 and owned by the same family since 1491, it has remained virtually unchanged for the last three hundred years. After the failure of the last Jacobite Rebellion, the gates at the top of the old drive were closed with the promise that they would not be reopened until a Stuart was back on the throne. The gates have remained closed ever since. Traquair is seven miles east of Peebles.

LOOK OUT FOR

The **bridge over the river in Langholm** (DG13 0JH) where the celebrated civil engineer Thomas Telford worked as an apprentice stonemason. His mark can be found on a pier on the far bank. Telford was born not far away and never forgot his roots. Behind the town hall is **Langholm's old library**, which he endowed with a grant of £1,000 in 1843. Immediately opposite the entrance is a stone doorway (set against a freestanding wall), which Telford carved when he was learning his stonemason's skills. If you're not stopping, at least give the great man a salute as you pass through.

WHERE TO STAY

The Gordon Arms (TD7 5LE) in the Yarrow Valley. A welcoming, old coaching inn in the middle of nowhere, with good rooms, an enticing menu and a fair chance of some live music.

Border House B&B (DG13 0JH) is in the middle of Langholm. Tidy rooms, good breakfast and they'll lock your bike up in the garage overnight.

WHERE TO EAT

Fletchers (TD7 4BA), by the filling station on the A7 as you leave Selkirk. A typical roadside café, painted a lurid colour, but serving no-nonsense food and getting you back on the road quickly and without fuss.

PRONUNCIATION LIST

Abriachan: Abb-*ree*-ah-chan (as in a*ch*tung)

Achiltibuie: Achilty-*Bew*-y (think a*ch*tung)

Aonach Mor: Oonnach *More* (ch as in a*ch*tung)

Ardgour: Ard-*gower*

Arrochar: *Arro*-cha (ch like clearing a fishbone from the back of the throat)

Assynt: *Ass*-int

Avoch: Och (ch as in a*ch*tung)

Ayr: Air

Bad a' Ghaill: Badda-haal (with a slight throat–clear on the 'h')

Ballachulish: Balla-*hoo*-lish

Ballantrae: Ballan-*tray*

Ballater: *Ballat*-er

Bealach na Ba: Bay-alluch na-bar (ch as in a*ch*tung)

Beauly: *Bew*-ly

Bellochantuy: Bella-can-*tee*

Bemersyde: Beemer-side

Berwick: *Berr*-ick

Birsay: *Burr*-sy

Braco: *Brake*-oh

Braemar: Bray-*mar*

Brechin: *Bree*-chin (ch as clearing a fishbone)

Brodgar: *Brod* -yar

Broughton: *Braw*-ton

Buachaille Etive Mor: Boo-er-challa Etive More (ch as in a*ch*tung)

Buccleuch: Buck-*cloo*

Burghead: Berg-head

Cappercleuch: Capper-*cloo*-ch (as in a*ch*tung)

Ceannabeinne: K'yawn na Ben-ye

Ciste Dubh: Kistya-doo

Cluanie: Cloo-annie

Coigach: *Koy*-gach (ch as in a*ch*tung)

Colintraive: Colin-*try*-ve

Cortachy: *Core*-ter-hee

Coupar Angus: Cooper *Angus*

Craigellachie: Craig-*ell*-achy

Crawick: Croy-k

Crieff: Kreef

Cuillins: *Coo*-linns

Culzean: Cull-*ain*

Daliburgh: *Dalli*-burra

Dalry: Dal-*rye*

Dawyck: Doy-k

Denholm: *Den*-num

Drumelzier: Drum-*elly*-ur

Drumnadrochit: *Drum*-na-*droch*-it

Dunrossness: Dun-*ross*-ness

Ecclefechan: Ekle-*fech*-an

Eigg: Egg

Eilean Donan: *Ay*-lan Don-an

Ellenabeich: Ellen-a-baych (ch as in a*ch*tung)

Eoropaidh: Yor-o-pee

Eradour: Era-*do-urr*

Eshaness: *Aish*-ness

Feochan: Fee–yoch-an (think a*ch*tung)

Findochty: Fin-*ech*-ty

Fionnphort: *Finna*-fort

Gigha: Gear

Glamis: Glaa'hms

Gourock: *Goo*-r'ck

Grandtully: *Grant*-ly

Gruinard: Grin-yard

Hawick: Hoy-k

Hourn: Hoo-urn

Houton: *How*-ton (rhymes with 'cow')

Inveraray: Inver-*airy*
Inverinate: Inver-*in*-nut
Jedburgh: *Jed*-burra
Jura: Jew-*ra*
Katrine: *Kat*-rinn
Kindardine: Kin-*card*-inn
Kingoldrum: Kin-*gold*-rum
Kirkcudbright: Kir-*koo*-bree
Kirkcaldy: Kir-coddy
Knockandhu: Knock-can-*doo*
Kyleakin: Kyle-*ack*-in
Kylerhea: Kyle-*ray*
Kylesku: Kyle-*skoo*
Langholm: *Lang*-um
Lerwick: *Lerr*-wick
Lesmahagow: Les-ma-*hay*-go
Leverburgh: *Lee*-va-burra
Lhanbryde: Lan-bride
Loch Beinn a' Mheadhain:
Loch Benn-a-*vey*-an
Loch nan Uamh: Loch nan Oo-av
Lochailort: Loch-*eye*-lort
Lyness: *Lie*-ness
Maeshowe: Maize-how
Meiklour: Me-*cloor*
Mòine Mhòr: Moyna-*More*
Moniaive: Money-I've
Moulin: *Moo*-lyn
Muthill: *Mew*-thil
Myreton: *Myre*-ton
Neidpath: *Need*-path
Orphir: *Or*-fur
Pennicuik: *Penny*-cook
Quiraing: Kwirr-*ang*
Quoyloo: Kwai-*loo*
Reiss: Reece
Roghadal: rhymes with 'yodel'
Samye Ling: Sammy-Ling

Sandness: *Sann*-ess
Sanquhar: *Sank*-er
Scone: Skoon
Scourie: *Skow*-rie
Seil: Seal
Sheil: Shee'll
Shiehallion: Shi-*hally*-on
Sleat: Slate
Sligachan: *Shlig*-uh-chan (as in a*ch*tung)
Spean Bridge: *Spee*-un *Bridge*
Stac Pollaidh: Stack Polly
Stoer: Stow-er
Strachur: Strach-*urr* (ch as in a*ch*tung)
Stranraer: Stran-*raar*
Strathaven: *Stray*-ven
Strontian: *Stron*-ti-un
Suilven: *Sool*-ven
Taynuilt: Tay-*nult*
Tighnabruaich: Tinna-*brew*-ich
(as in a*ch*tung)
Tioram (Castle): Cheerum
Tomintoul: Tom-in-*towel*
Tore: rhymes with 'more'
Traquair: Track-*ware*
Tyndrum: Tyne-*drum*
Tynron: *Tin*-run
Uig: *Oo*-ig
Uist: *Yew*-ist
Unst: Uh-nst (as in 'Unstable')
Urquhart: *Urch*-urt (ch as in a*ch*tung)
Wamphray: *Wom*-fri
Wideford: *Wide*-ford

USEFUL ADDRESSES AND INFORMATION

ABOUT SCOTLAND

VisitScotland is Scotland's national tourist board. It has a comprehensive website with information about visitor attractions, accommodation, and events. It also has a useful 'Practical Information' section dealing with passports requirements, consulate addresses, and FAQs.
www.visitscotland.com

Undiscovered Scotland is a privately run blend of visitor guide, accommodation finder and business directory. It's packed with information and, once you've mastered it, you'll probably be a regular visitor. To find out about places you're planning to visit, navigate to Discover and click on the area map. Every black dot has an interesting page behind it.
www.undiscoveredscotland.co.uk

FERRIES

The Hebrides, and islands in the Firth of Clyde
Caledonian MacBrayne (a.k.a. CalMac) | www.calmac.co.uk
0800 066 5000

Gourock – Dunoon
Western Ferries
www.western-ferries.co.uk
01369 704452

Cromarty – Nigg (summer only)
Highland Ferries
www.highlandferries.co.uk
07468 417137

Glenelg – Skye (Easter – October only)
Skye Ferry CIC | www.skyeferry.co.uk
NB Advance booking not required.
Payment by cash only.

Orkney (External)
Northlink Ferries
www.northlinkferries.co.uk
0845 6000 449

Pentland Ferries
www.pentlandferries.co.uk
01856 831 226

Orkney (Inter-island)
Orkney Ferries
www.orkneyferries.co.uk
01856 872044

Shetland (External)
Northlink Ferries
www.northlinkferries.co.uk
0845 6000 449

Shetland (Inter-island)
Shetland Islands Council
www.shetland.gov.uk/ferries
01595 745804

ACCOMMODATION

Rooms

www.bikerbnb.co.uk – it's early days for this Scottish-based site which is still building up its database. It promises to find biker-friendly and biker-suitable accommodation in Scotland and beyond.

www.privatehousestays.com is an easy to use website listing owner-occupied B&Bs in Scotland. A good selection of hand-picked properties across the price range.

www.visitscotland.com has an extensive directory of places to stay. As the country's official Tourist Board it also runs a national grading system to maintain standards.

Campsites

www.campsites.co.uk
www.pitchup.com

Campsites Apps

www.wikicamps.co.uk
Campmate (from Campsites.co.uk)

GENERAL INFORMATION

First aid

Get the First Aid app from the British Red Cross. Loads of advice that you can access without the need for a mobile signal or internet connection. Free, simple and life-saving. www.redcross.org.uk/first-aid/first-aid-apps

Ticks and their safe removal

www.lymediseaseaction.org.uk/about-ticks/tick-removal

Or www.highland.gov.uk/ticks

NC500 (website and app)

www.northcoast500.com

Recording your journey

The Polarsteps app automatically tracks your route and the places you visit along the way. It creates a travel record while you enjoy yourself.
www.polarsteps.com

Riding in a group?

Consider the Wolfpack app to help you organise, plan and communicate.
www.wolfpack.run

Road and travel information

www.trafficscotland.org

Weather forecast websites (with apps)

www.bbc.co.uk/weather
www.metoffice.gov.uk
www.yr.no (good info but you might need to change the language settings)

INDEX

PHOTOGRAPHY CREDITS

All photography © J.G.Fergusson, with the exceptions of:

Pages 16, 86 © Erik Peters

Pages 17 (top), 74, 89, 116, 124, 178, 191: © VisitScotland/ Kenny Lam

Pages 20, 30, 34, 76, 80, 166 and 168 © John Herbin

Page 24 (Beardmore Precision) © yesterdays.nl

Page 25 (Douglas advert) © London Douglas Motorcycle Club

Pages 25 (Jock Porter), 27 (Bob McIntyre) and 28 (Steve Hislop) © Mortons Archive

Page 26 (Jimmy Guthrie) © Castrol Archive

Page 26 (Fergus Anderson) © Artur Fenzlau/Technisches Museum Wien

Page 27 (Jock Taylor stamp) © Isle of Man Post Office

Page 30 (Loud Pipes!) © Daryll Cannon (killboy.com)

Pages 31, 57, 72 and 148 © Helen Strong

Pages 32, 114, 144, 162 and 172 © Shutterstock

Pages 42 and 58 © Jim Millington

Pages 46, 48, 56, 70, 73, 74, 88, 89, 96, 110, 114, 118, 120, 122, 156, 159, 160, 182, 183, 194 and Cover: © VisitScotland/ Paul Tomkins

Pages 78, 134, 136 and 146 © Motorcycle Diaries

Page 152 © Ken Amer

Page 158 © Dave Diamond

Page 167 © VisitScotland/Damian Sheilds

The author and publisher are grateful to all the photographers and picture libraries for their help in tracking down images and for their kind permission to reproduce them in these pages. If any photographs have been wrongly attributed, please accept our apologies and allow us to correct them in future editions.

Motorway
Trunk road
A road

0   50 km
0   30 miles

To Lerwick

Kirkwall

Lerwick

Durness
Thurso
Wick

Kylesku
Stornoway
Lochinver
Lairg
Ullapool

Gairloch

Dingwall
Banff
Peterhead

Portree
INVERNESS
Grantown
-on-Spey

Aviemore
Tomintoul
Banchory
ABERDEEN

Fort
Augustus
Braemar
Ballater
Stonehaven

Mallaig
Fettercairn

Fort
William
Pitlochry
Montrose

Tobermory
Arbroath
DUNDEE

Oban
PERTH
St Andrews
Crianlarich

Inveraray
Dunfermline
STIRLING
Dunbar

Lochgilphead
GLASGOW
EDINBURGH
Berwick
-upon-
Tweed

Castlebay

Peebles

Ayr
Hawick

Campbeltown
Moffat

Girvan
NEWCASTLE
UPON TYNE

Dumfries
SCOTLAND
ENGLAND

NORTHERN
IRELAND
Stranraer
Hexham

Larne
Carlisle
Durham

BELFAST
Penrith

© www.helenstirlingmaps.com 2018.
Contains Ordnance Survey Data
© Crown Copyright database right 2017